AF255196

Blessed Be . . .

Journaling thru the Beatitudes
with Illustrations to Color

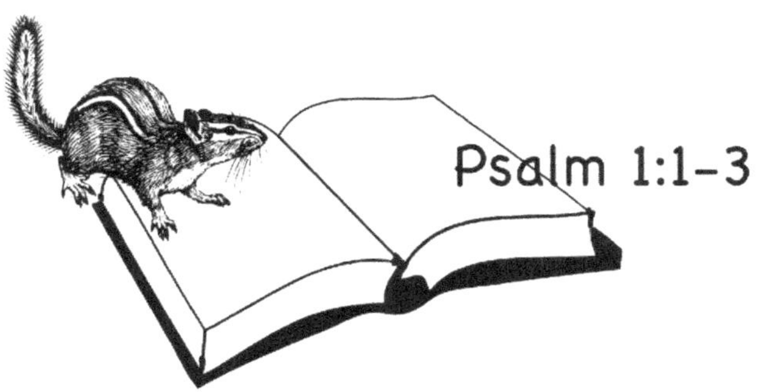

Isla W. Backus

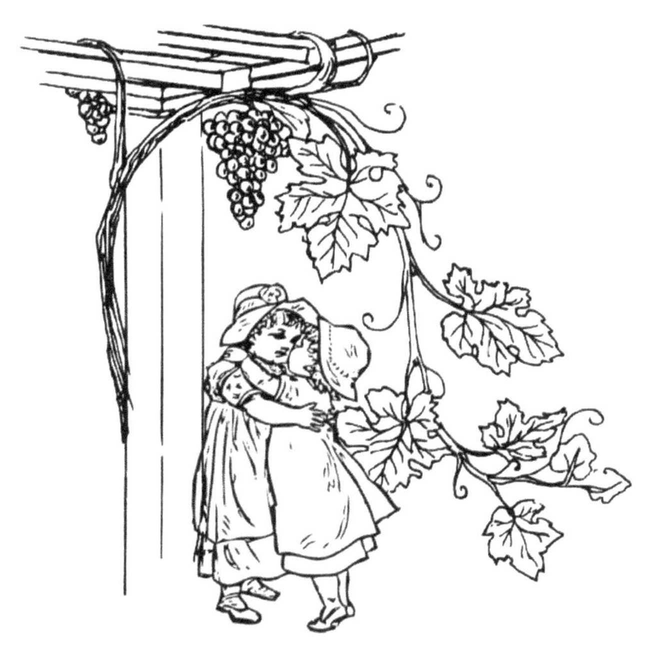

Dedicated to 'Isla, Jr.' and Lola
for their ongoing encouragement and
support. And to my beloved John
for his patience and his faith in me!

Using This Book

This book grew out of my recently discovered love of illustrating Bible passages as I study the Word. I found that I spent more time in meditation on verses, and gained greater insights, as I happily sketched and colored my way through my 'quiet times.'

So based on my experience, I have some recommendations for using this illustrated journal:

1) Read the associated verse(s) and the questions before you begin to color an illustration, and spend a moment in prayer for insight and wisdom.

2) Don't jump to answer the questions right away. Let your subconscious mind dwell on the verse as you color, and take your time. Don't feel that you have to finish the questions - or the coloring! - in one sitting. I've found it helpful to let the verses 'simmer' over time.

3) There is a page after each picture to allow you to record additional thoughts and observations you have had as you work.

4) Enjoy! Research has shown that coloring helps fight stress, encourage relaxation, and inspire calm and creativity.

It has always been my goal to have a positive impact on the life of every person I meet. With that thought in mind, I send out this small book with a simple prayer - that you might

Blessed be . . .
Isla

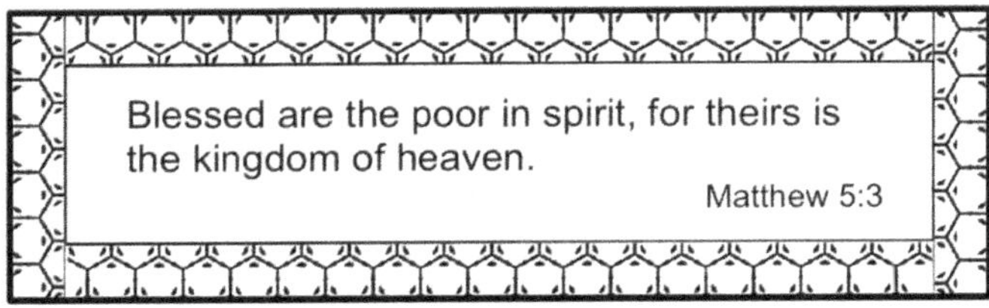

What does it mean to be poor in spirit?

What is the kingdom of heaven?

Why is it necessary to be poor in spirit in order to have the kingdom?

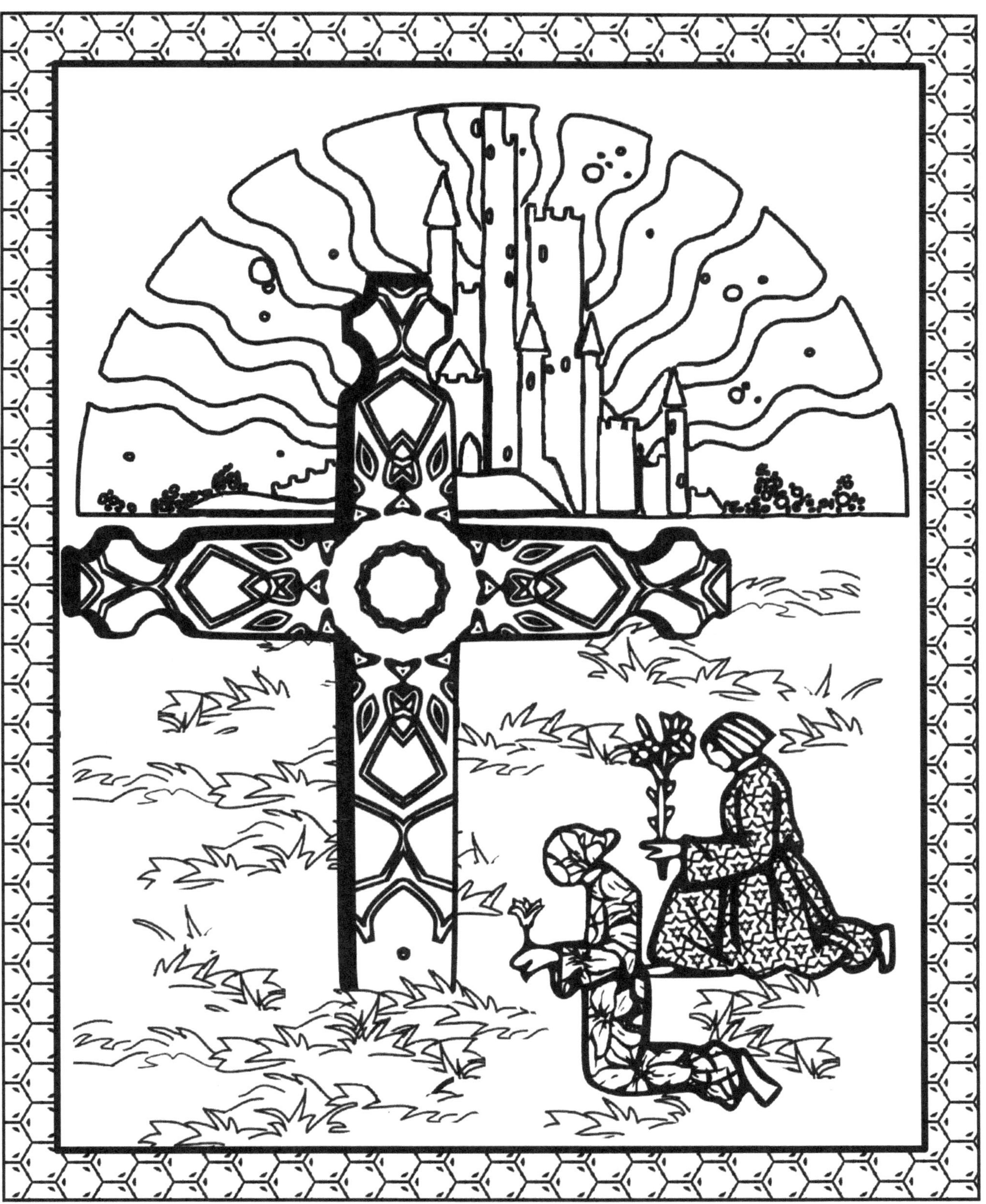

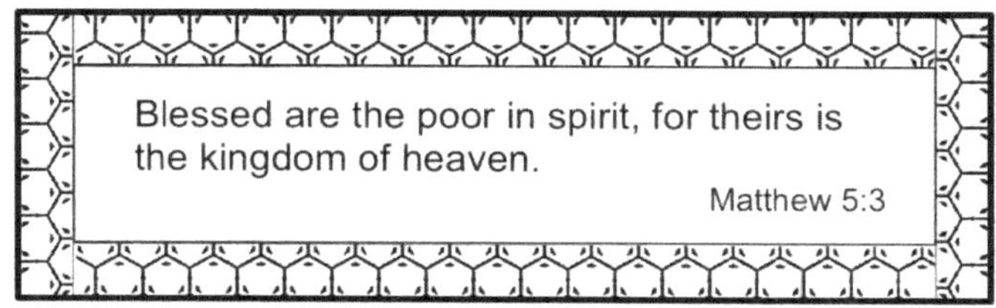

Further thoughts:

All these things my hand has made, and so all
these things came to be, declares the Lord, but
this is the one to whom I will look; he who is humble
and contrite in spirit and trembles at my word.
Isaiah 66:2

God has created everything - yet he looks for us. Why?

What does it mean to be humble and contrite in spirit?

If we tremble at His word, how does that affect our behavior?

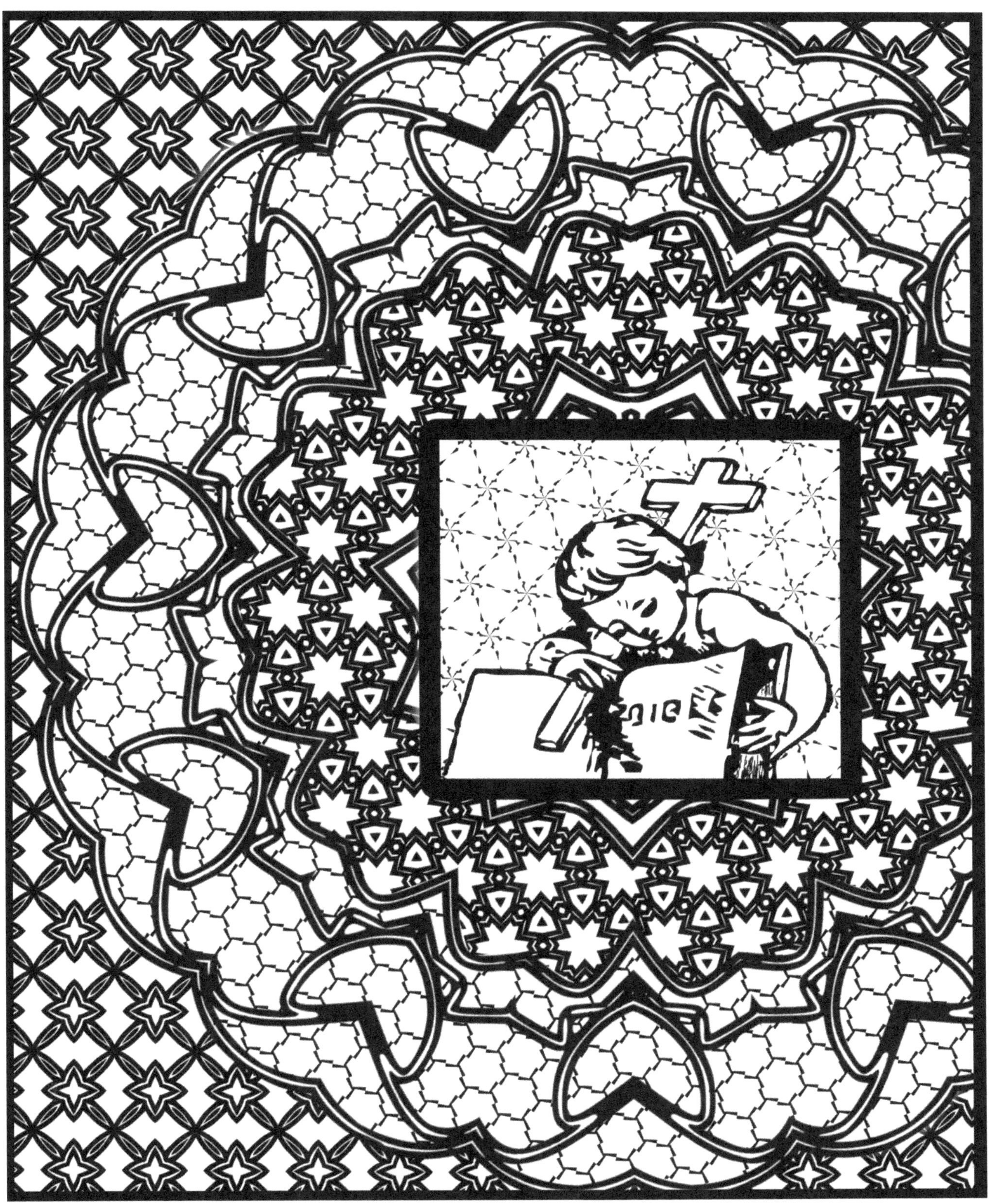

All these things my hand has made, and so all these things came to be, declares the Lord, but this is the one to whom I will look; he who is humble and contrite in spirit and trembles at my word.

Isaiah 66:2

Further thoughts:

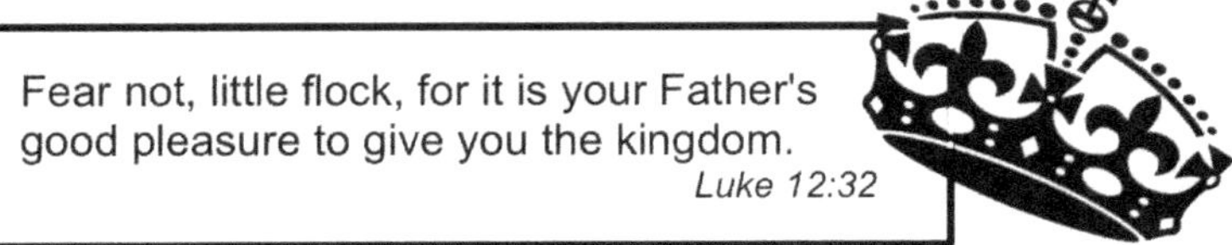

What fear is Christ addressing? And what fears do you face?

Who is in His flock? Why are they likened to sheep?

Why does it please God to give them the kingdom?

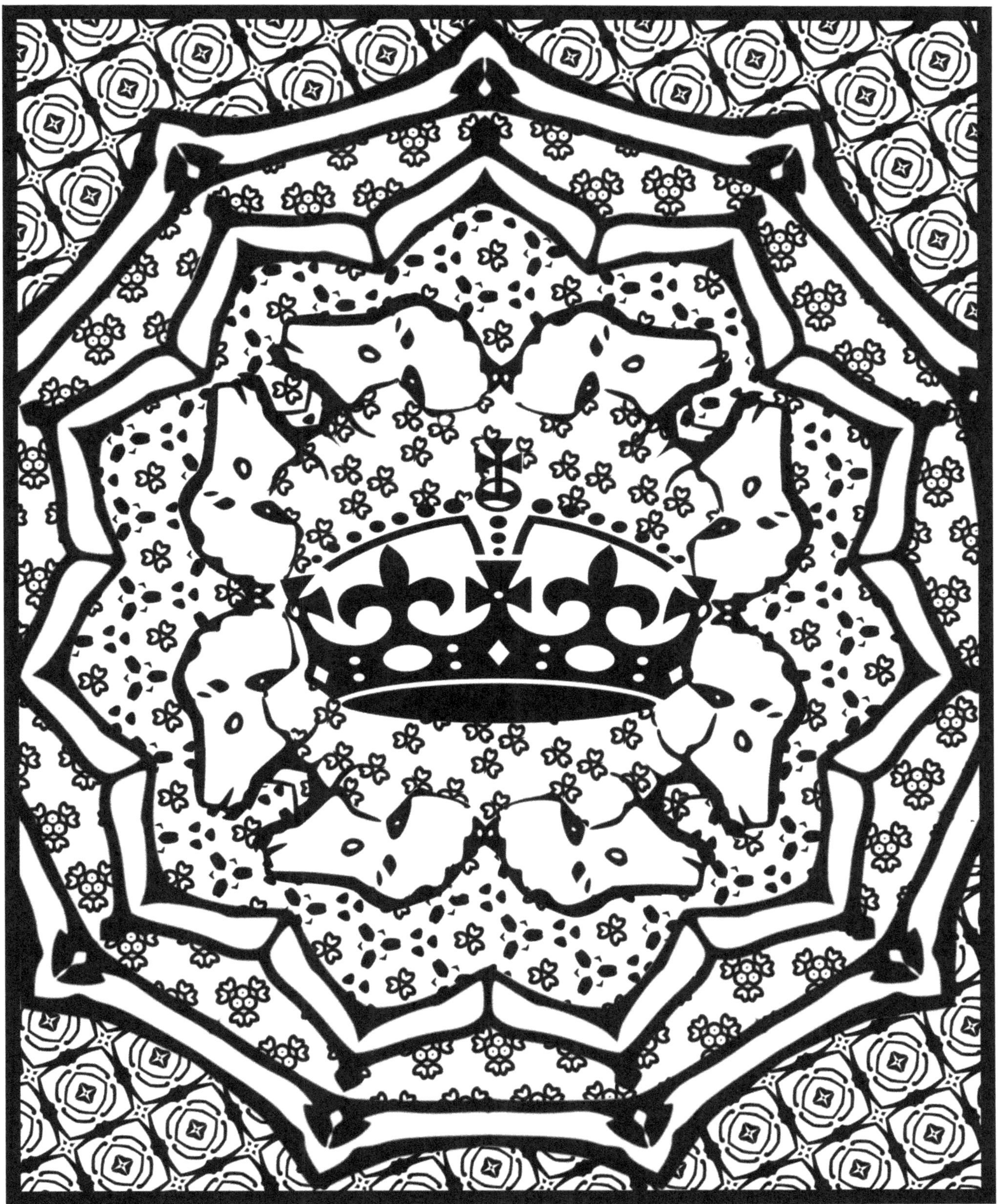

Further thoughts:

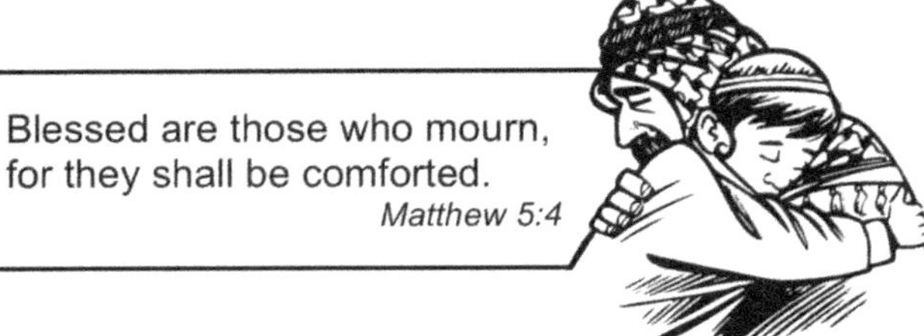

At some point in time, all people mourn. But contextually, Christ is singling out a particular group of mourners. What, then, do these people mourn?

What is the source of comfort for this kind of grief?

Do you think Christ is referring only to comfort in heaven? Or here and now as well?

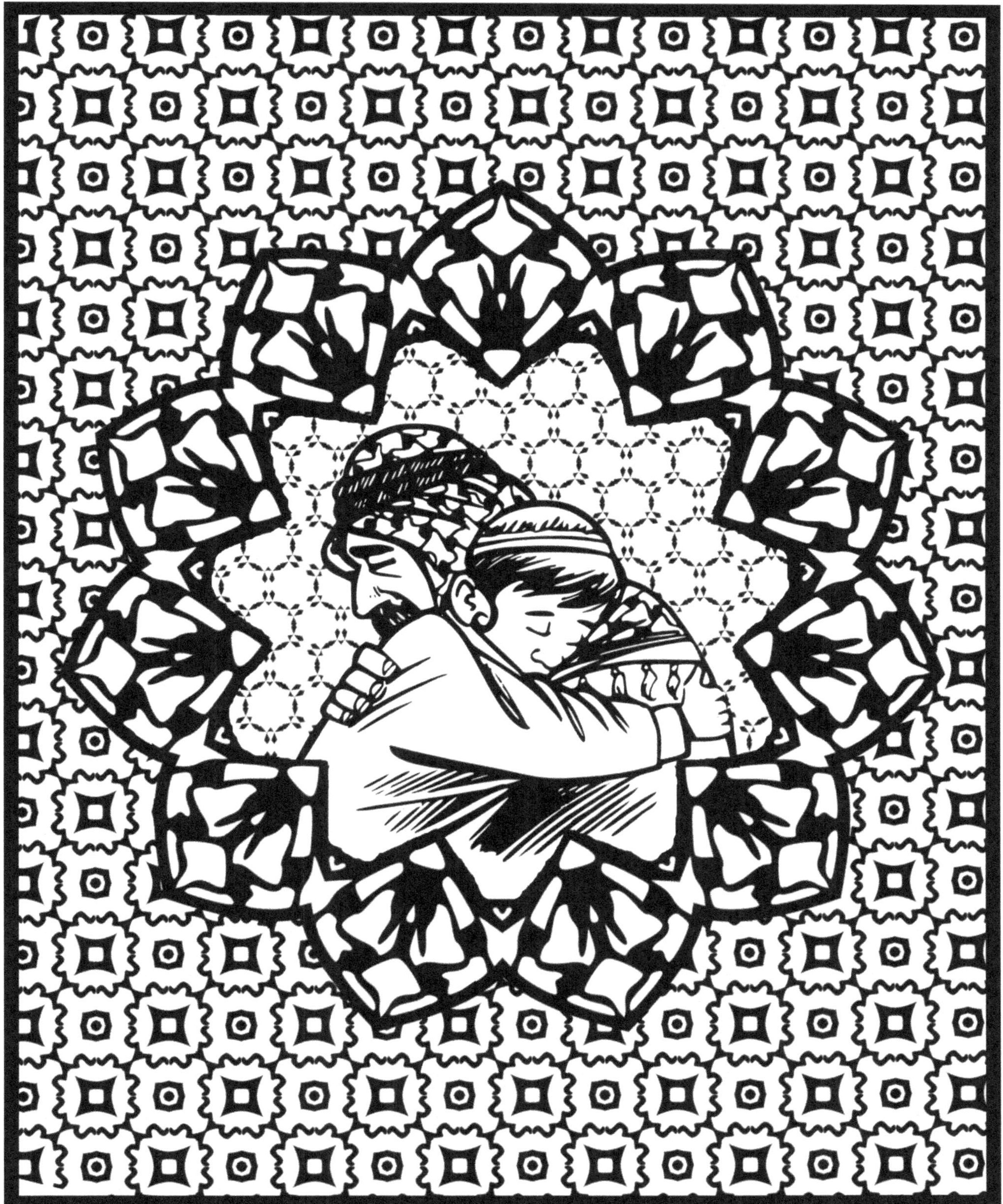

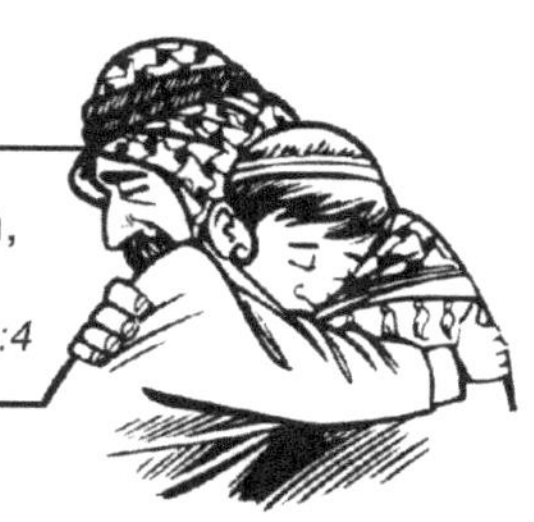

Further thoughts:

He will wipe away every tear from their eyes,
and death shall be no more, neither shall there
be mourning, nor crying, nor pain anymore,
for the former things have passed away.

Revelation 21:4

Notice the 'negatives' in this verse - no more death, no more mourning, no more crying, no more pain. Why are they listed seperately? Are they all synonymous, listed only for emphasis? Or is each one distinct and different?

If each is distinct, what differentiates them?

How do you feel this verse relates to Matthew 5:4?

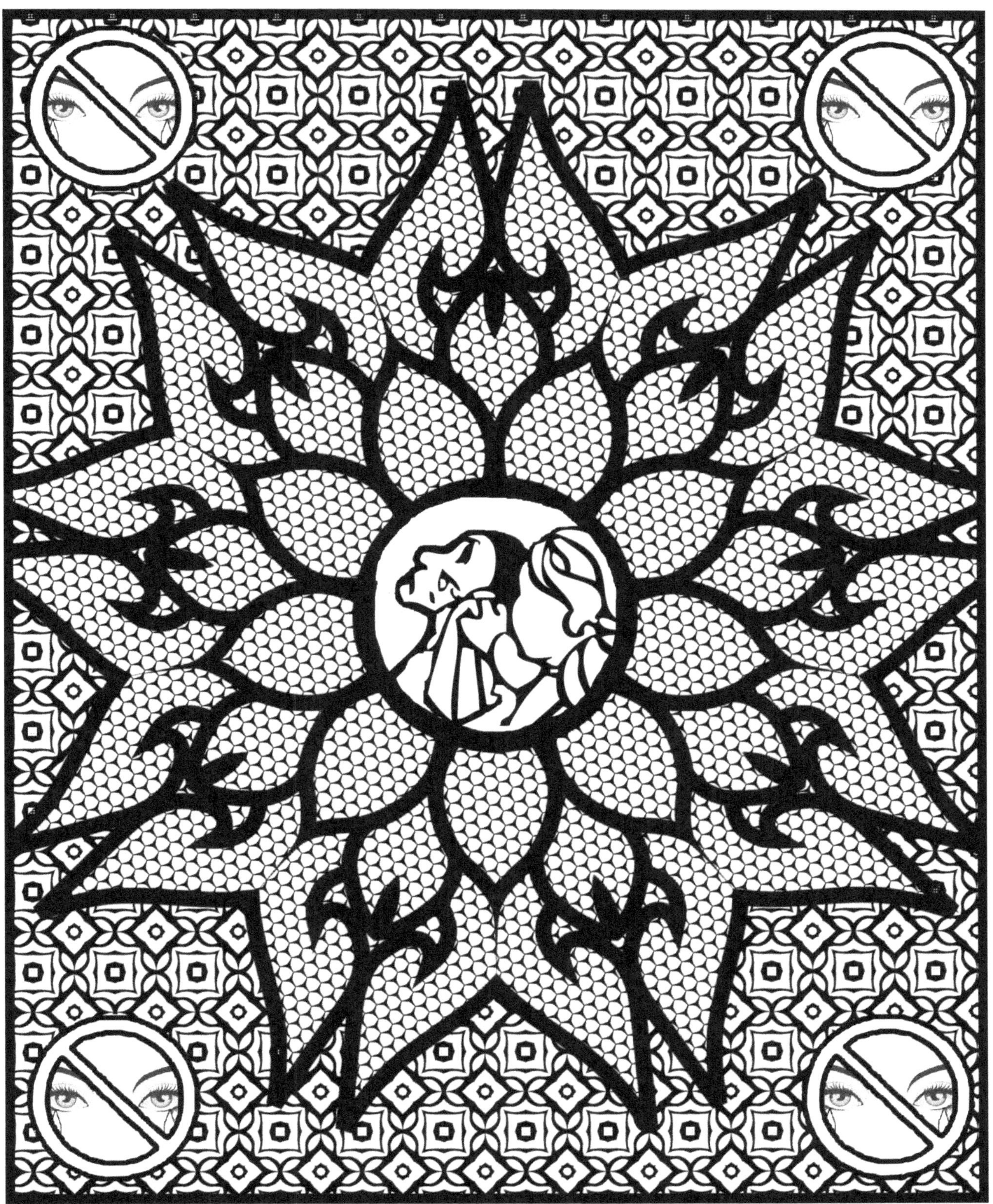

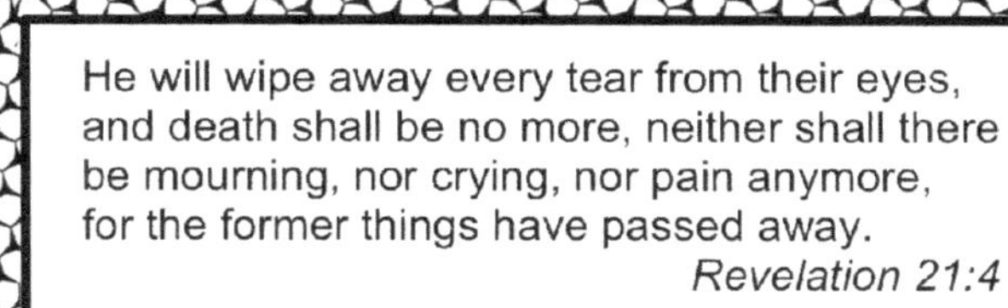

Further thoughts:

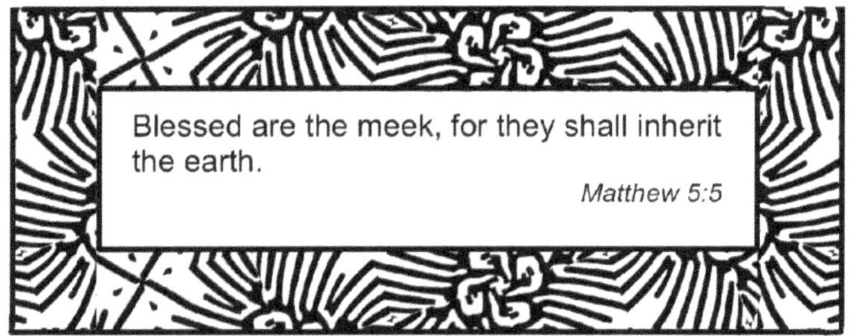

What does it mean to be meek?

What will it mean to inherit the earth?

How will the earth be different? How will our oversight of the earth be different than it is now?

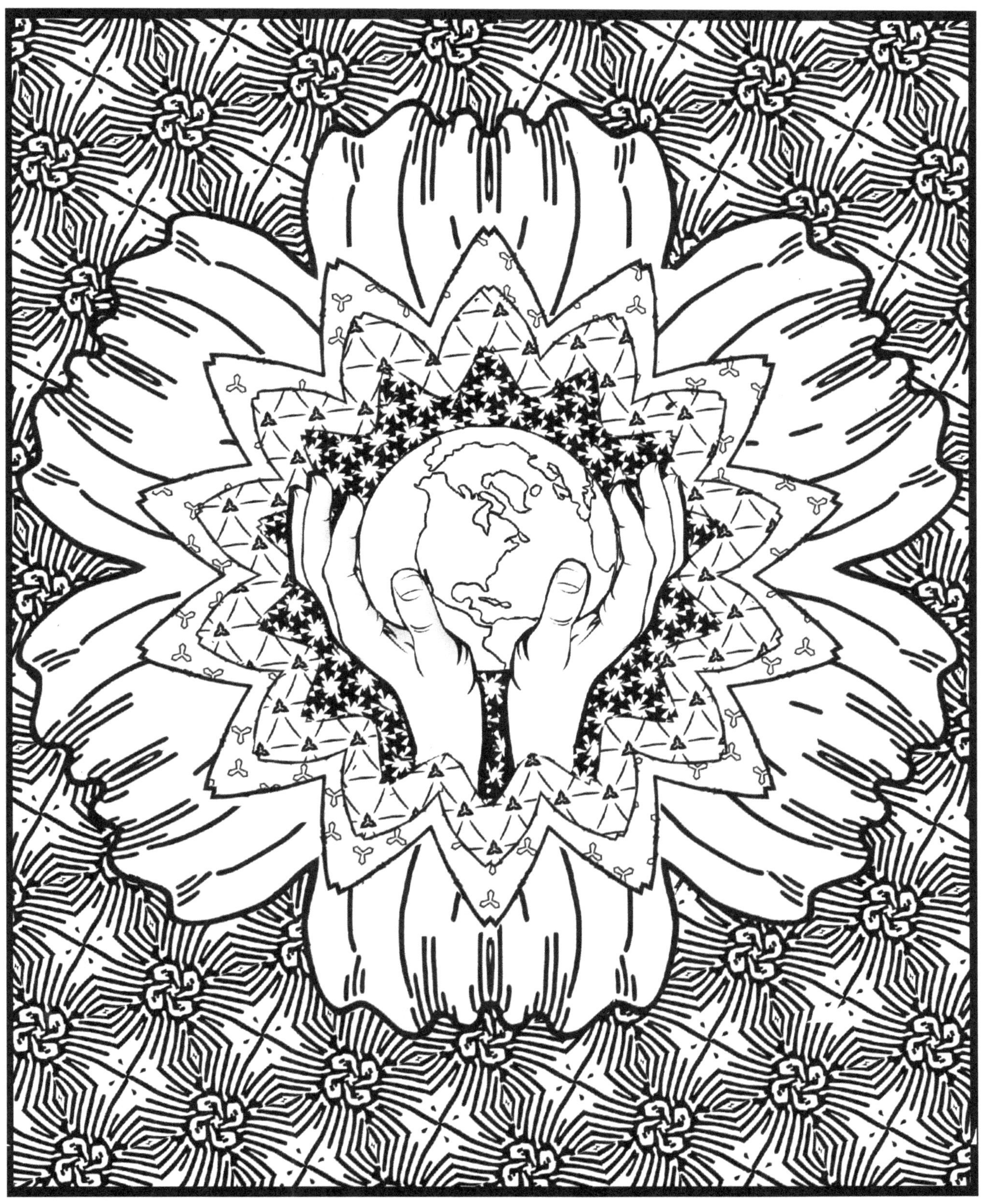

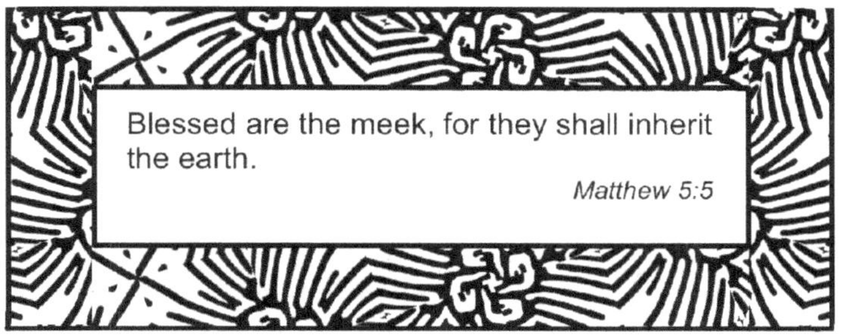

Further thoughts:

Refrain from anger, and forsake wrath! Fret not yourself; it tends only
to evil. For the evildoers shall be cut off, but those who wait for the Lord
shall inherit the land. In just a little while, the wicked will be no more;
though you look carefull at his place, he will not be there. But the meek
shall inherit the land and delight themselves in abundant peace.

Psalm 37:8-11

What is the connection between anger (or wrath) and evil?

What does it mean to wait for the Lord?

What do you think it will be like to "delight yourself in abundant peace?"

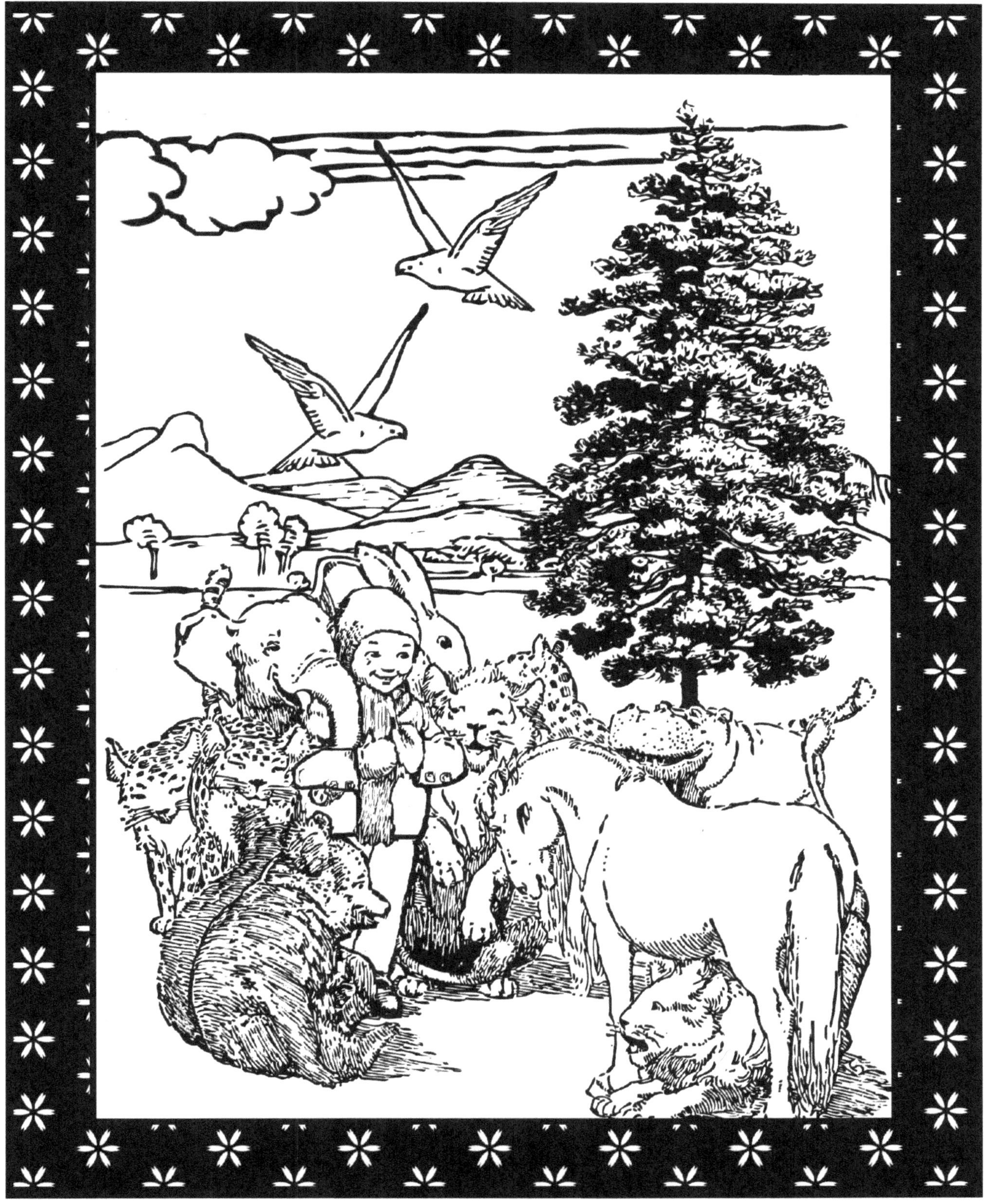

Refrain from anger, and forsake wrath! Fret not yourself; it tends only
to evil. For the evildoers shall be cut off, but those who wait for the Lord
shall inherit the land. In just a little while, the wicked will be no more;
though you look carefull at his place, he will not be there. But the meek
shall inherit the land and delight themselves in abundant peace.

Psalm 37:8-11

Further thoughts:

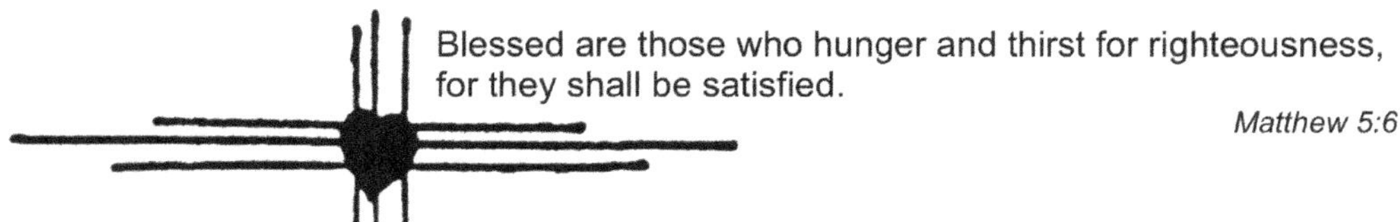

How can we cultivate a hunger and thirst for righteousness?

How would such a hunger and thirst change your life?

What is righteousness, anyway?

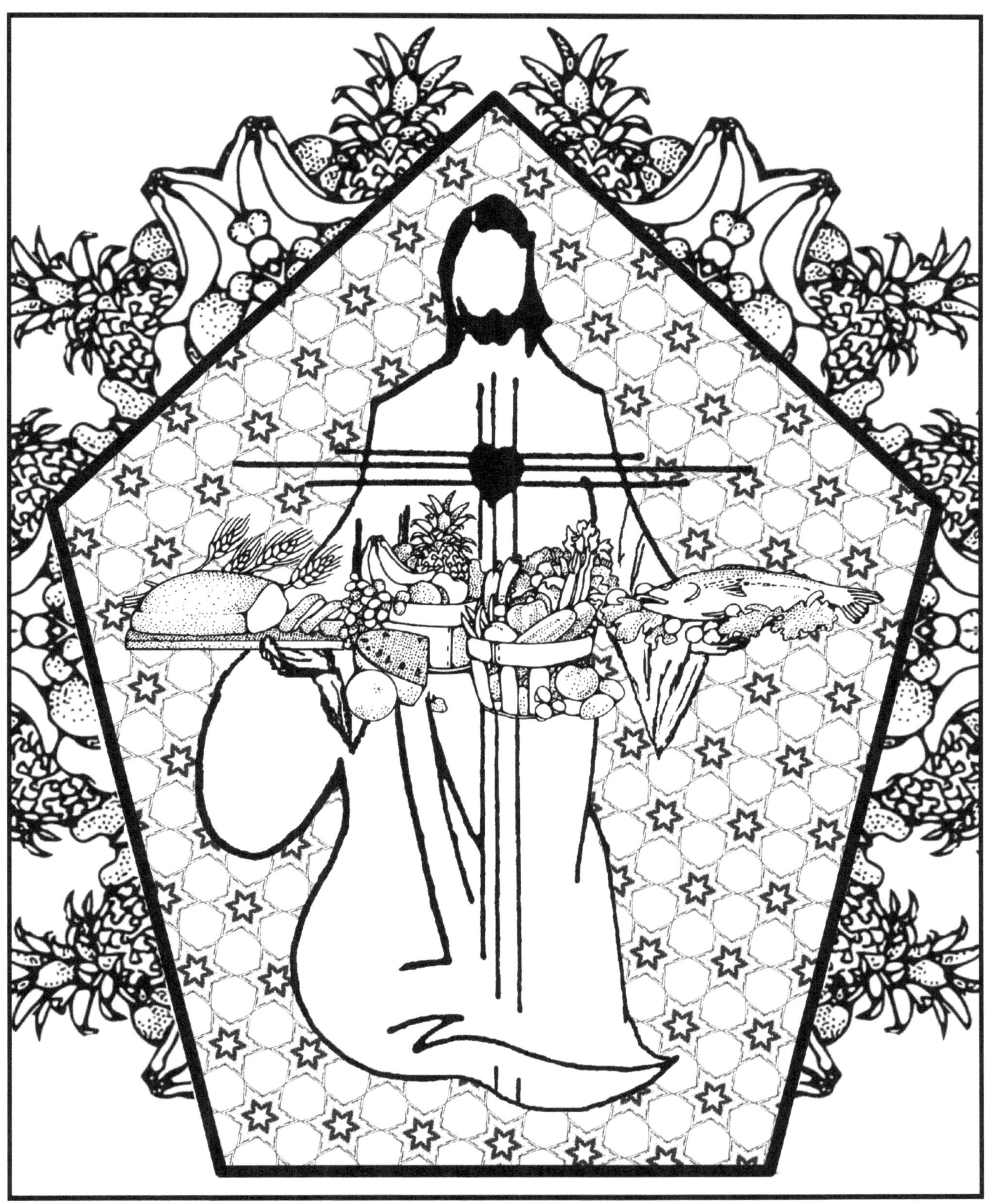

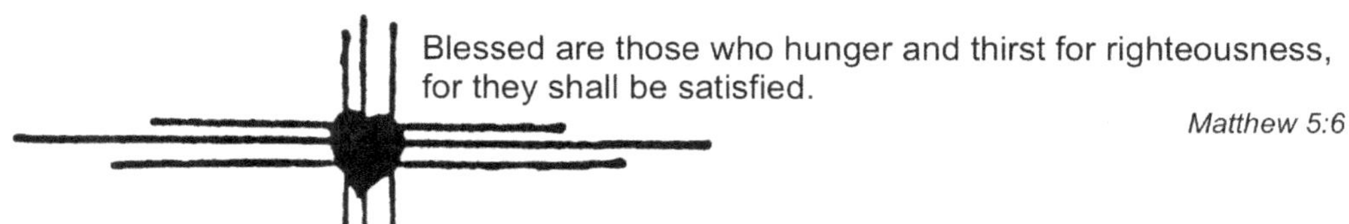

Further thoughts:

Blessed is the man who walks not in the counsel of the wicked,
nor stands in the way of sinners, nor sits in the seat of scoffers;
but his delight is in the law of the Lord and on his law he meditates
day and night. He is like a tree planted by streams of water that
yields its fruit in its season, and its leaf does not wither. In all
that he does, he prospers.

Psalm 1:1-3

How does meditation on God's law influence our behavior?

God likens this person to a fruitful tree. What type of 'fruit' would your tree yield?

Does the promise of prosperity apply only to financial success? What other areas might we prosper in?

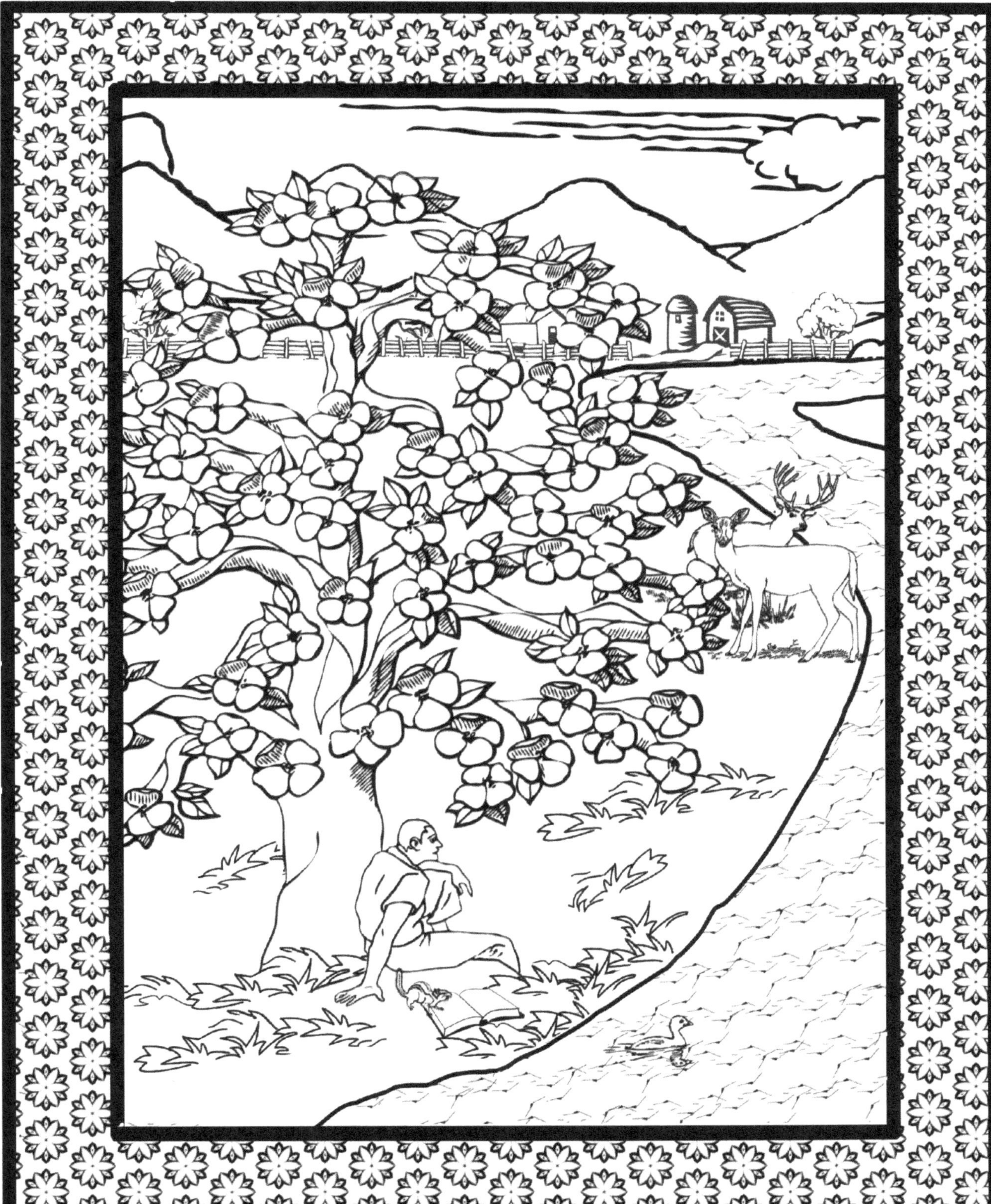

Blessed is the man who walks not in the counsel of the wicked, nor stands in the way of sinners, nor sits in the seat of scoffers; but his delight is in the law of the Lord and on his law he meditates day and night. He is like a tree planted by streams of water that yields its fruit in its season, and its leaf does not wither. In all that he does, he prospers.

Psalm 1:1-3

Further thoughts:

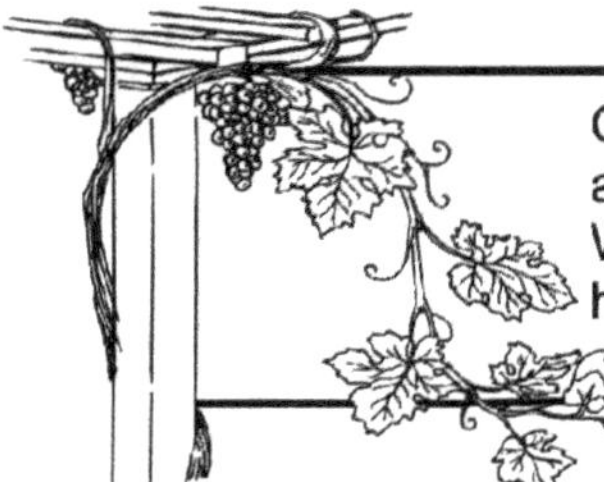

On the last day of the feast, the great day, Jesus stood up and cried out, "If anyone thirsts, let him come to me and drink. Whoever believes in me, as the Scripture has said, 'Out of his heart will flow rivers of living water.'"

John 7:37-38

What type of thirst is Jesus talking about? What are people thirsting for?

How does someone drink from Jesus?

What does Jesus mean by 'living water?'

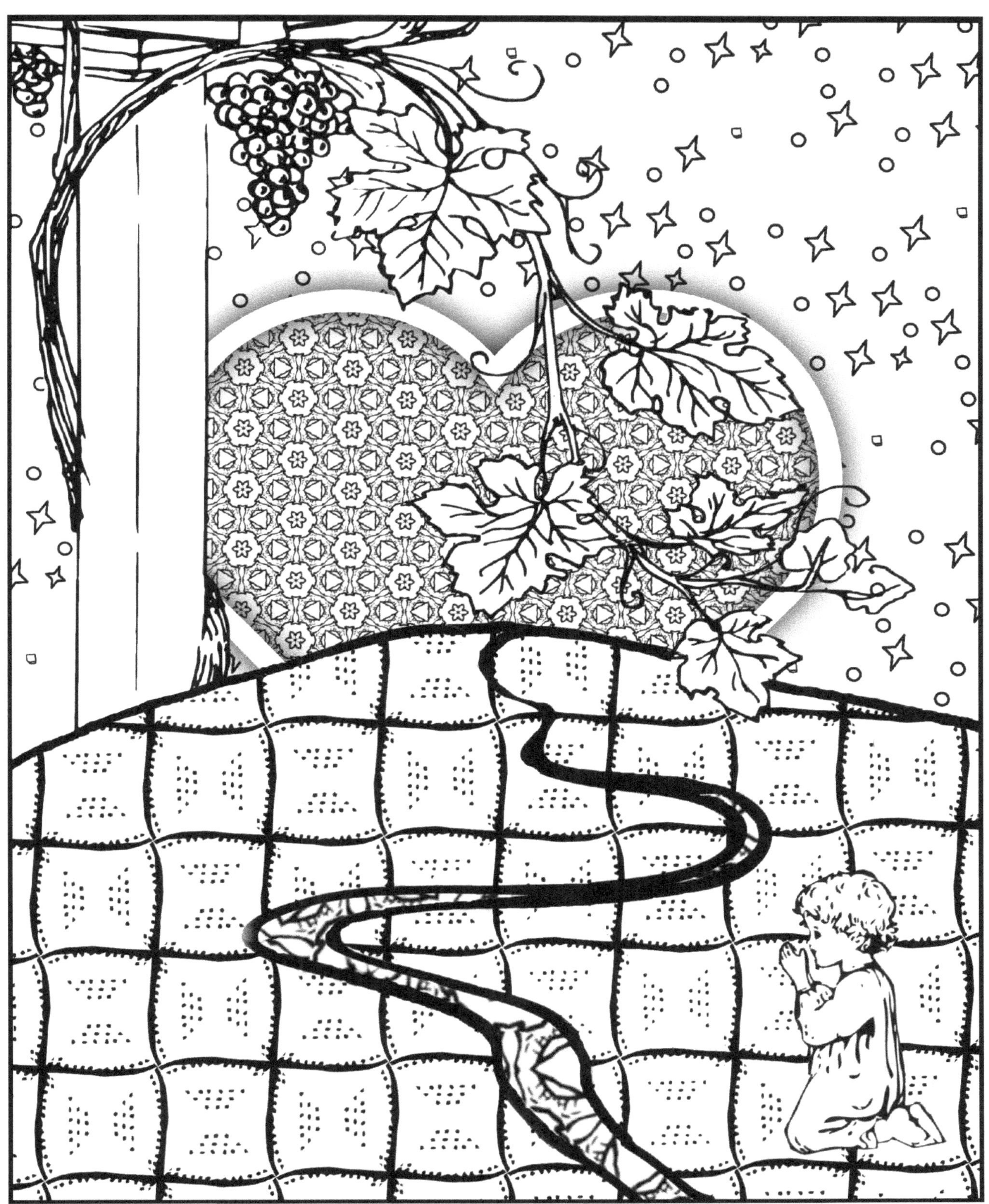

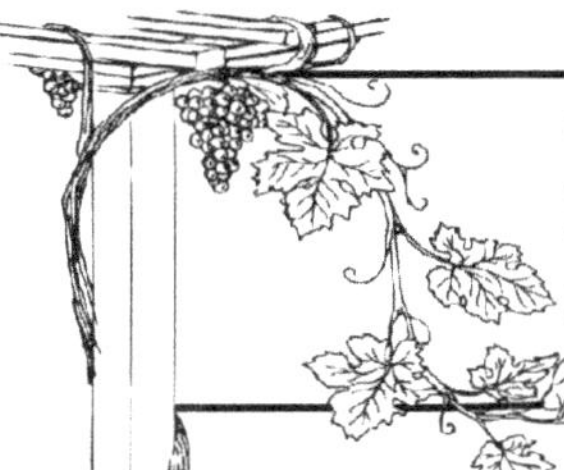

On the last day of the feast, the great day, Jesus stood up and cried out, "If anyone thirsts, let him come to me and drink. Whoever believes in me, as the Scripture has said, 'Out of his heart will flow rivers of living water.'"

John 7:37-38

Further thoughts:

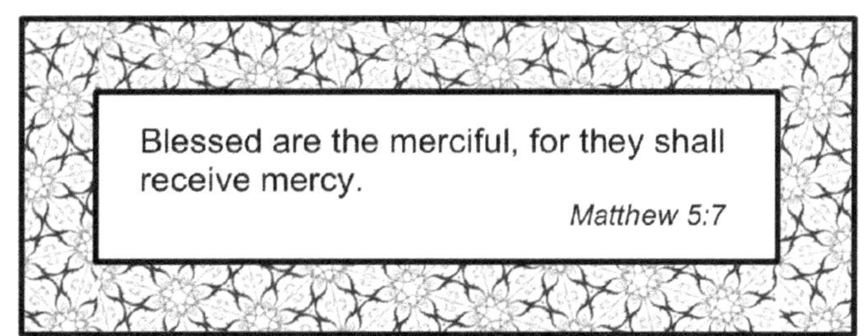

What does it mean to be merciful?

Are there specific situations in your life where you have the opportunity to show mercy?

Why do you **need** mercy from God in your life?

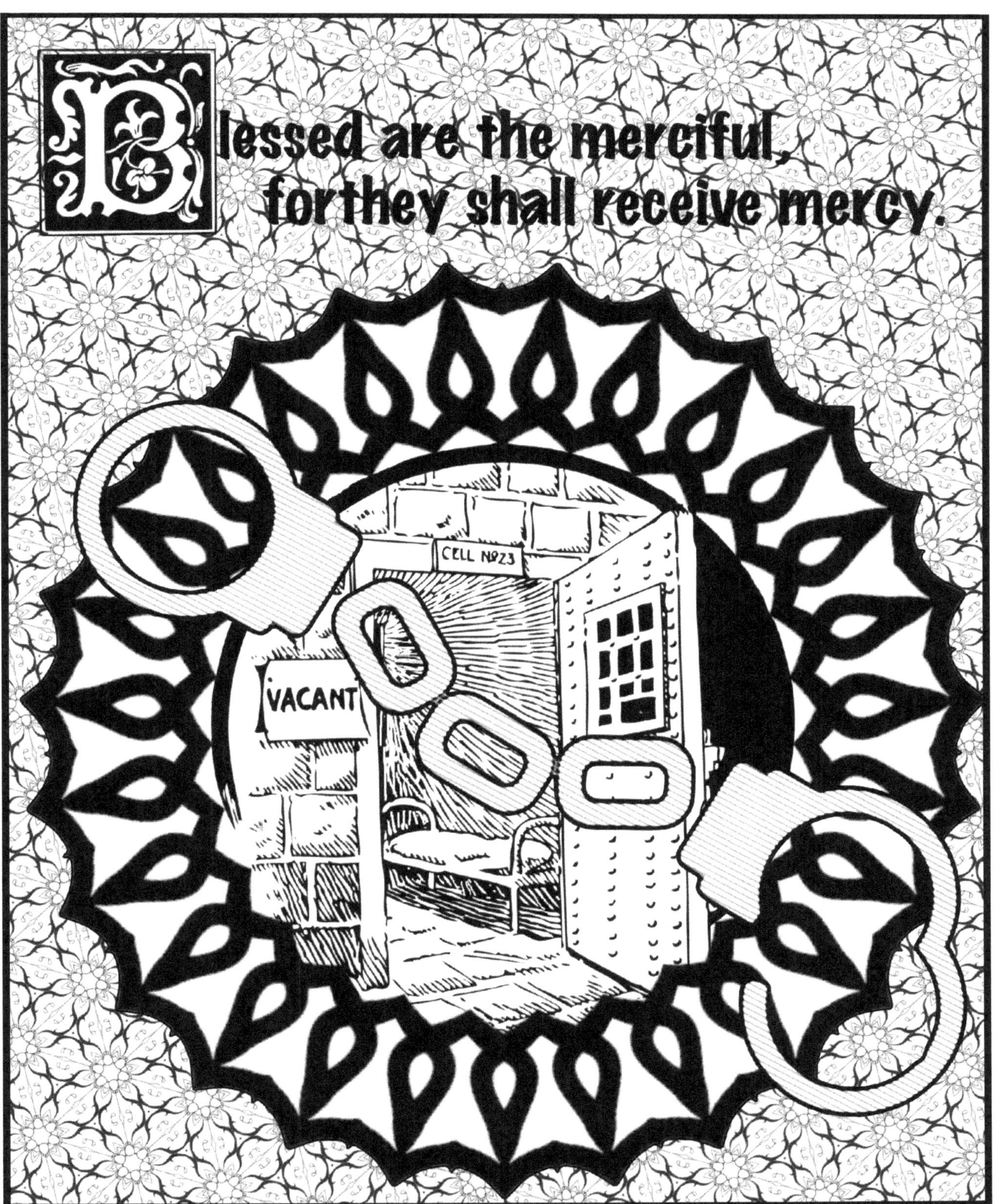

Blessed are the merciful,
forthey shall receive mercy.
CELL N?23
VACANT

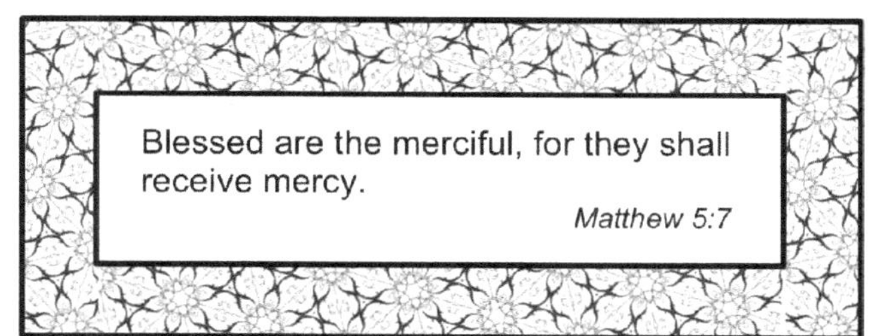

Further thoughts:

> Then the King will say to those on his right, "Come, you who are blessed by my Father, inherit the ingdom prepared for you from the foundation of the world. For I was hungry and you gave me food, I was thirsty and you gave me drink, I was a stranger and you welcomed me, I was naked and you clothed me, I was sick and you visited me, I was in prison and you came to me."
>
> *Matthew 25:34-36*

What is significant about the fact that these people are on Jesus' right?

What makes these verses good companion verses to Matthew 5:7?

Did you notice that the kingdom has been <u>prepared</u> for you? What does that mean?

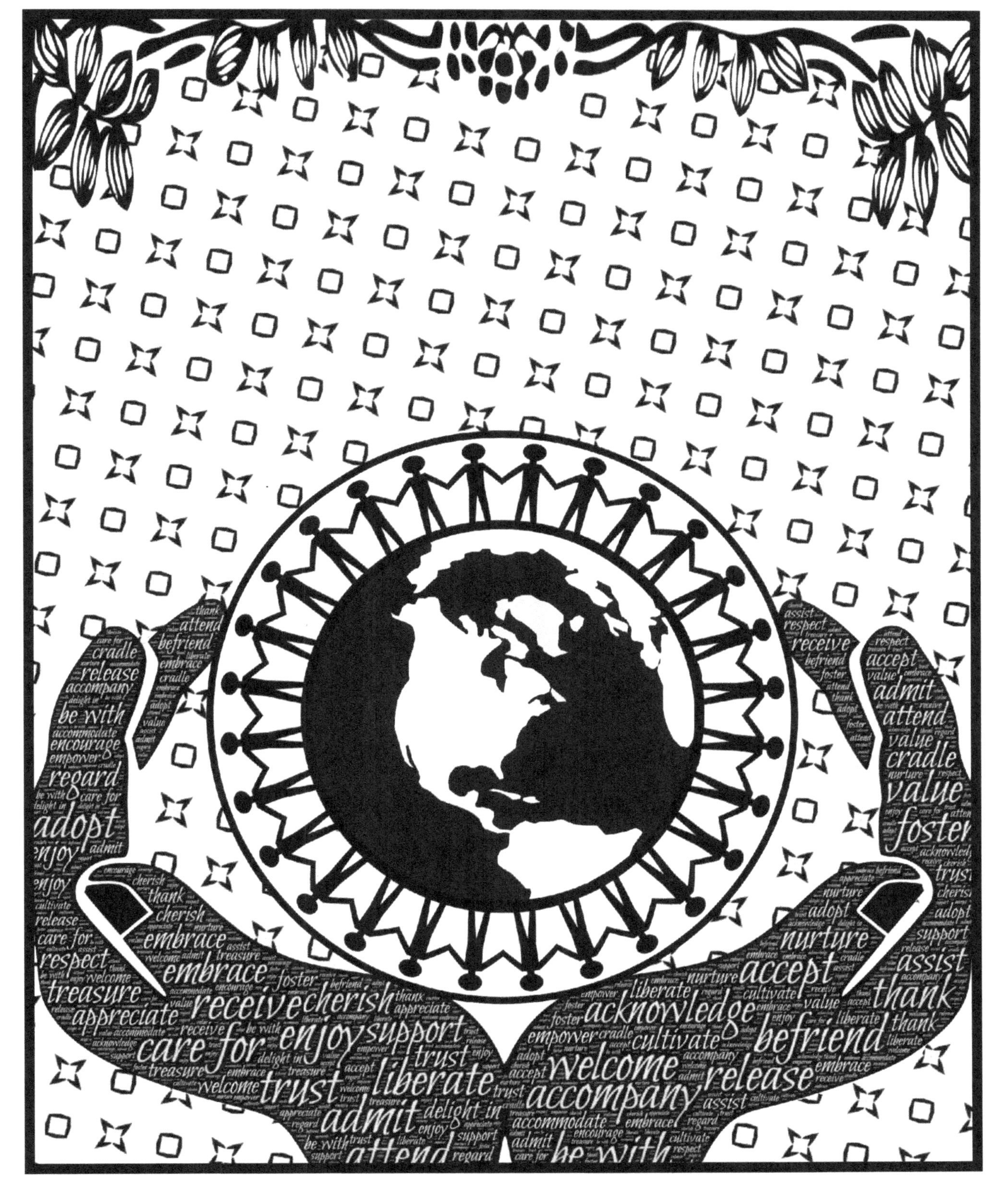

Then the King will say to those on his right, "Come, you who are blessed by my Father, inherit the ingdom prepared for you from the foundation of the world. For I was hungry and you gave me food, I was thirsty and you gave me drink, I was a stranger and you welcomed me, I was naked and you clothed me, I was sick and you visited me, I was in prison and you came to me."

Matthew 25:34-36

Further thoughts:

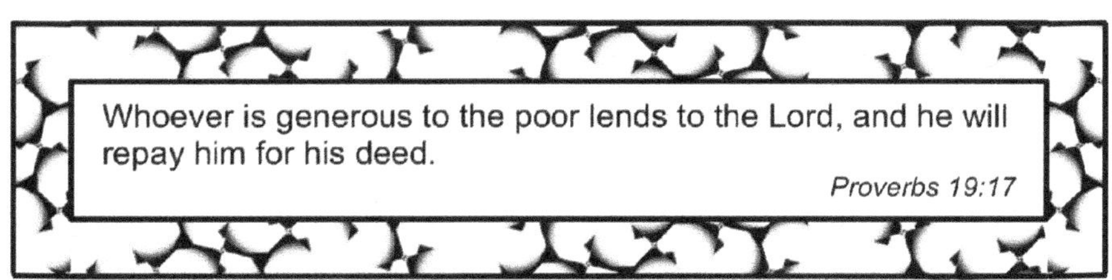

How does one measure generosity? By our own comfort level? In proportion to the need?

A loan (as opposed to a gift) implies interest will accrue on the balance due until repayment is made. So the loan becomes a source of profit for the lender. How do we profit by lending to God?

When can we expect repayment on such a loan? And what form will that repayment take?

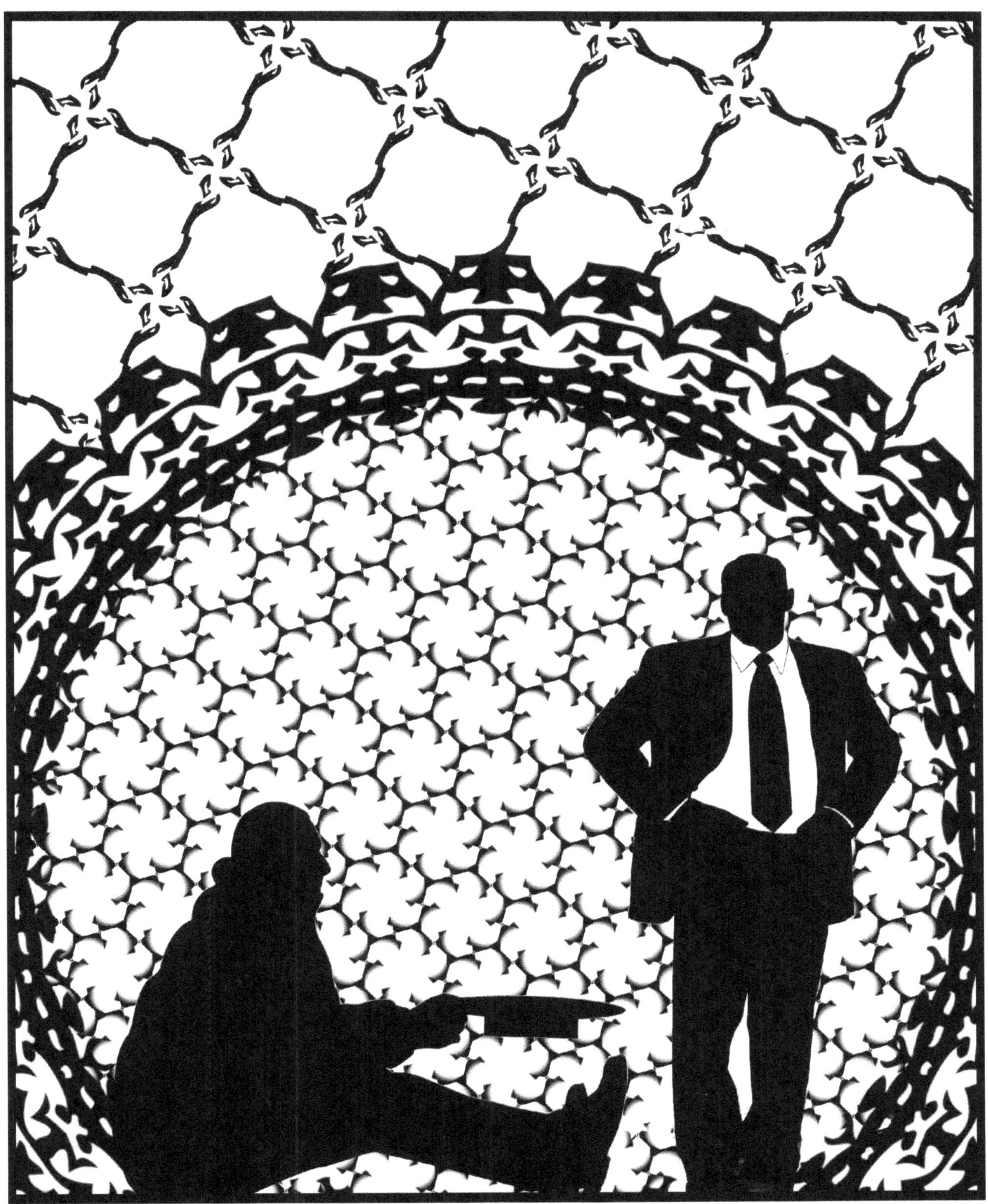

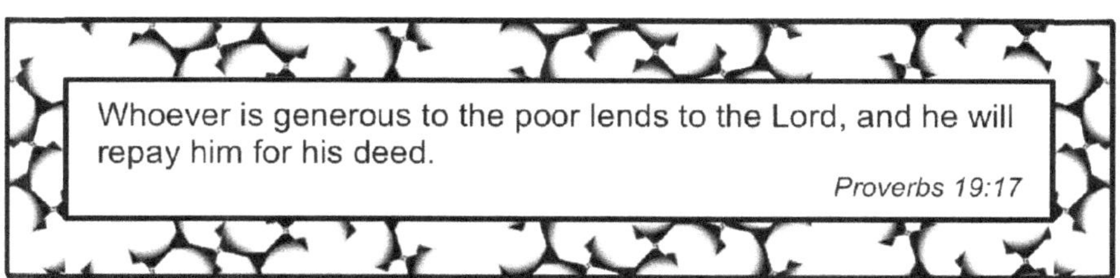

Further thoughts:

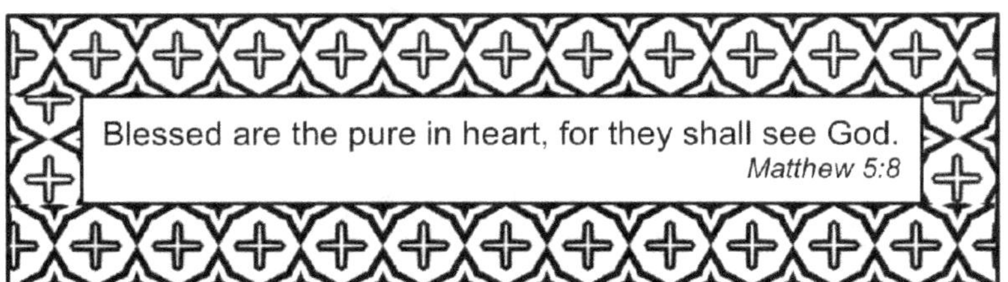

What does it mean to be pure in heart?

How do we achieve - much less retain - a pure heart?

Are there specific things in your life that make it more difficult to maintain a pure heart? How can you deal with these things more effectively?

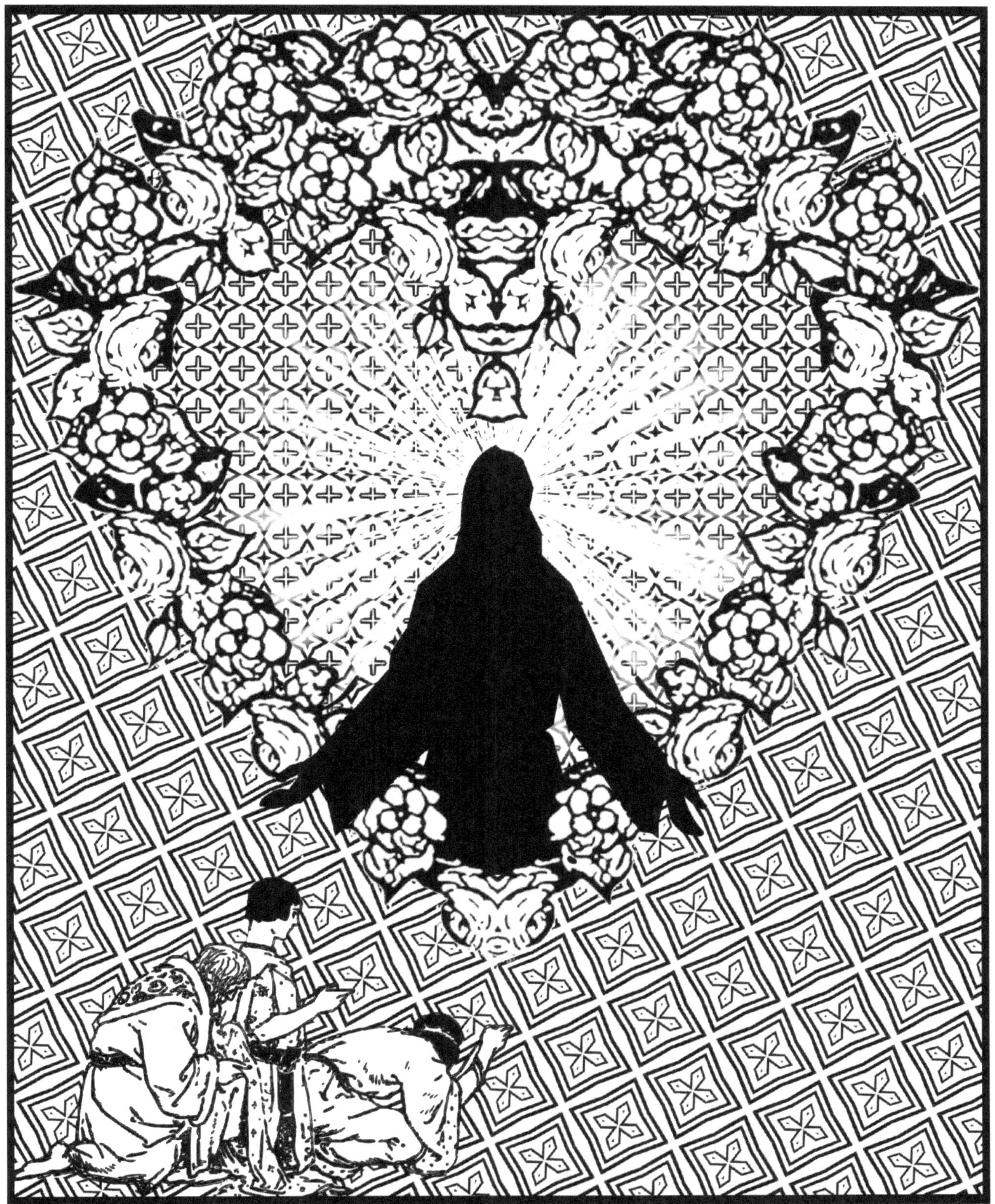

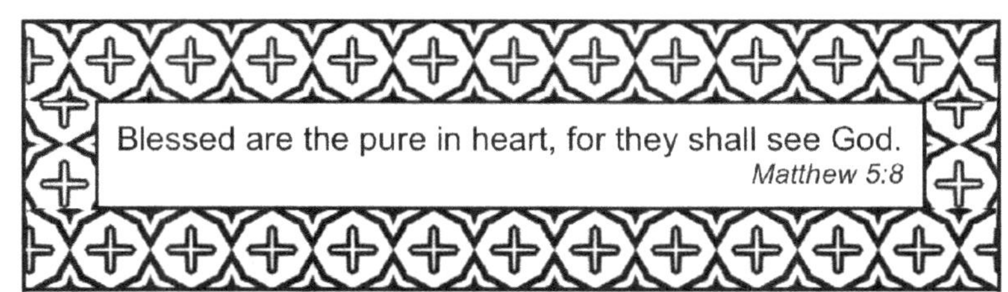

Further thoughts:

Who shall ascend the hill of the Lord? And who shall stand in his holy place?
He who has clean hands and a pure heart, who does not lift up his soul to
what is false and does not swear deceitfully. He will receive blessing from
the Lord and righteousness from the God of his salvation.

Psalm 24:3-5

Clean hands may refer to right actions. A pure heart to righteous motivation. And the rest to righteousness in our speech. If we can keep true to these principles, how will the world around us be different?

Where do you think the hill of the Lord and His holy place are located? Can we reach them without His help?

Righteous actions, righteous motivation, and righteous speech - all are required. Yet the verse indicates that righteousness is given by God. How does this paradox relate to our salvation?

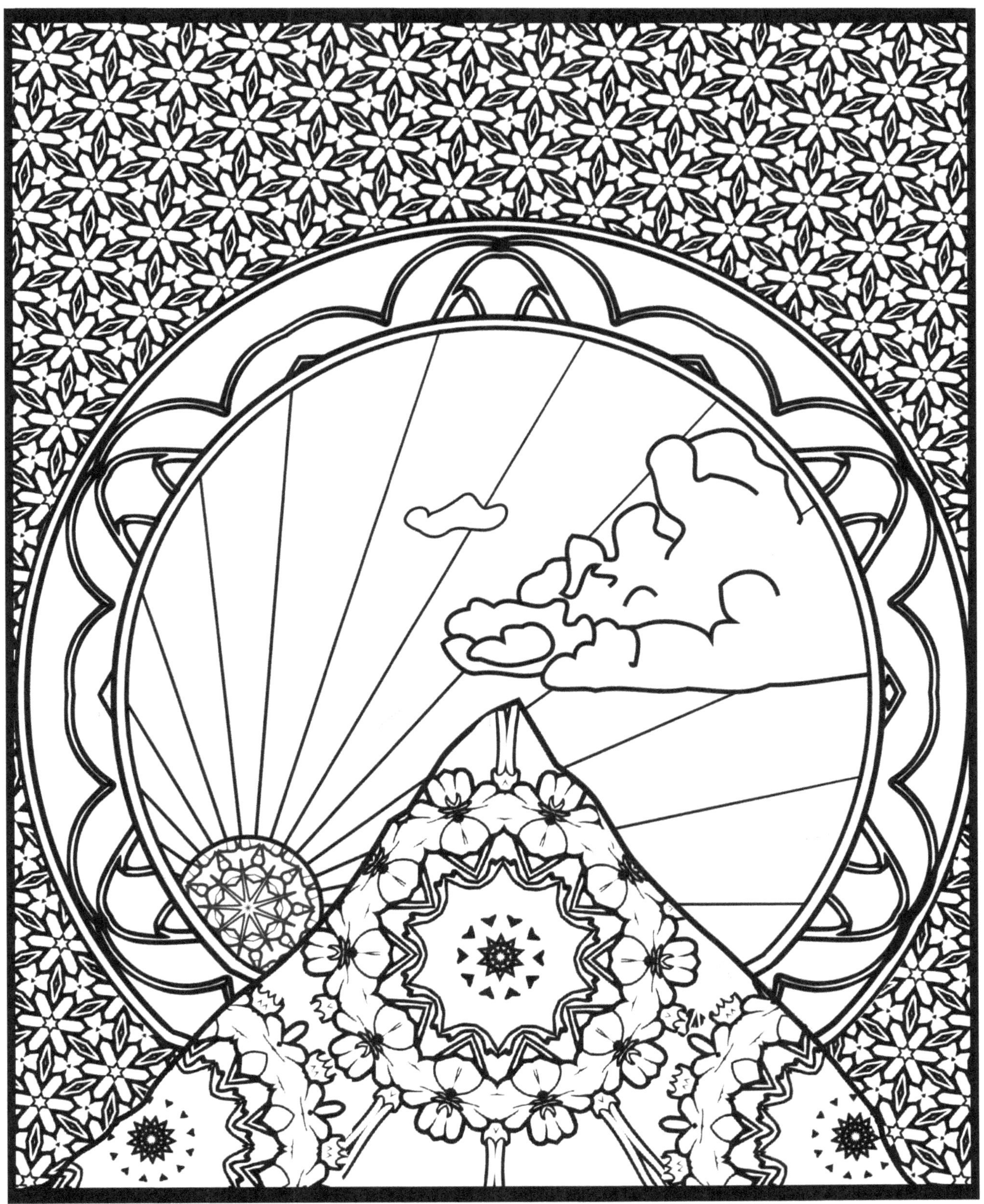

Who shall ascend the hill of the Lord? And who shall stand in his holy place?
He who has clean hands and a pure heart, who does not lift up his soul to
what is false and does not swear deceitfully. He will receive blessing from
the Lord and righteousness from the God of his salvation.

Psalm 24:3-5

Further thoughts:

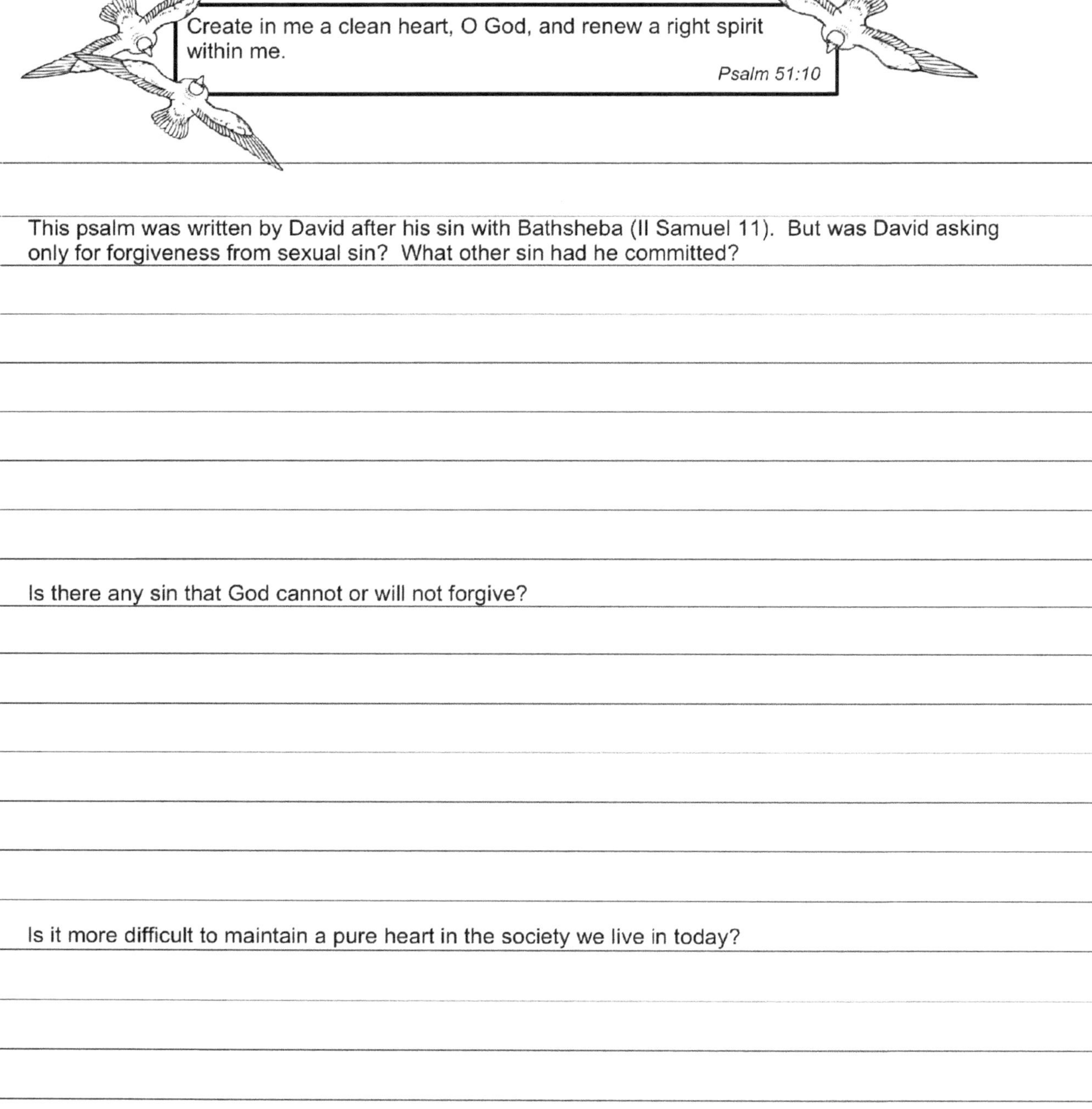

This psalm was written by David after his sin with Bathsheba (II Samuel 11). But was David asking only for forgiveness from sexual sin? What other sin had he committed?

Is there any sin that God cannot or will not forgive?

Is it more difficult to maintain a pure heart in the society we live in today?

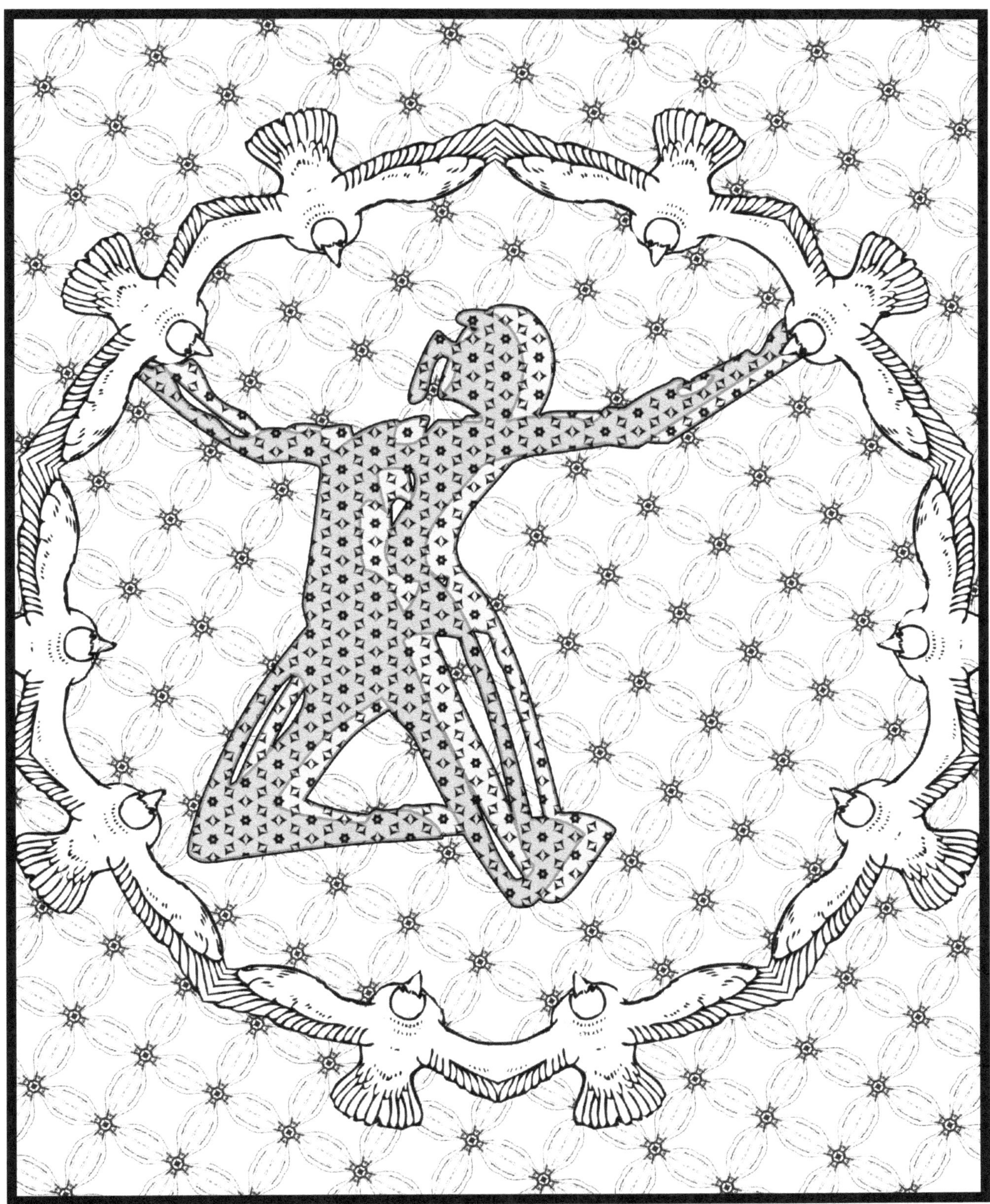

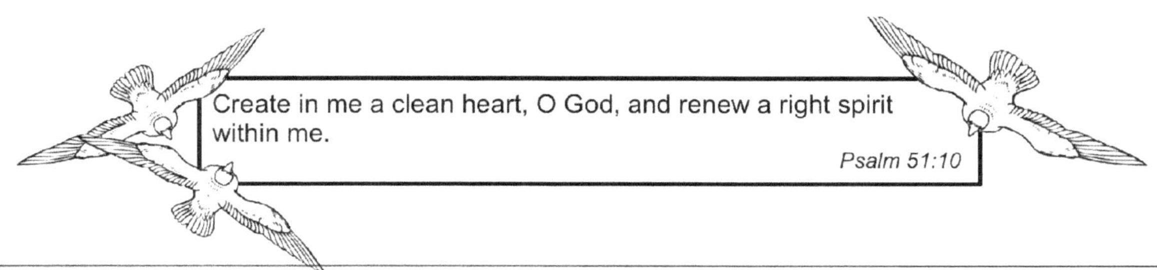

Further thoughts:

Blessed are the peacemakers, for they shall be called the sons of God.

Matthew 5:9

Notice that these do not simply live in peace - they actually *make* peace. What *actions* can you take to promote peace in your life and your relationships?

Are you in conflict with anyone now? How can you be a peacemaker in this situation?

God's Son gave his life to bring peace between God and man. Is this mission of reconciling men to God part of the task of the peacemaker referred to here?

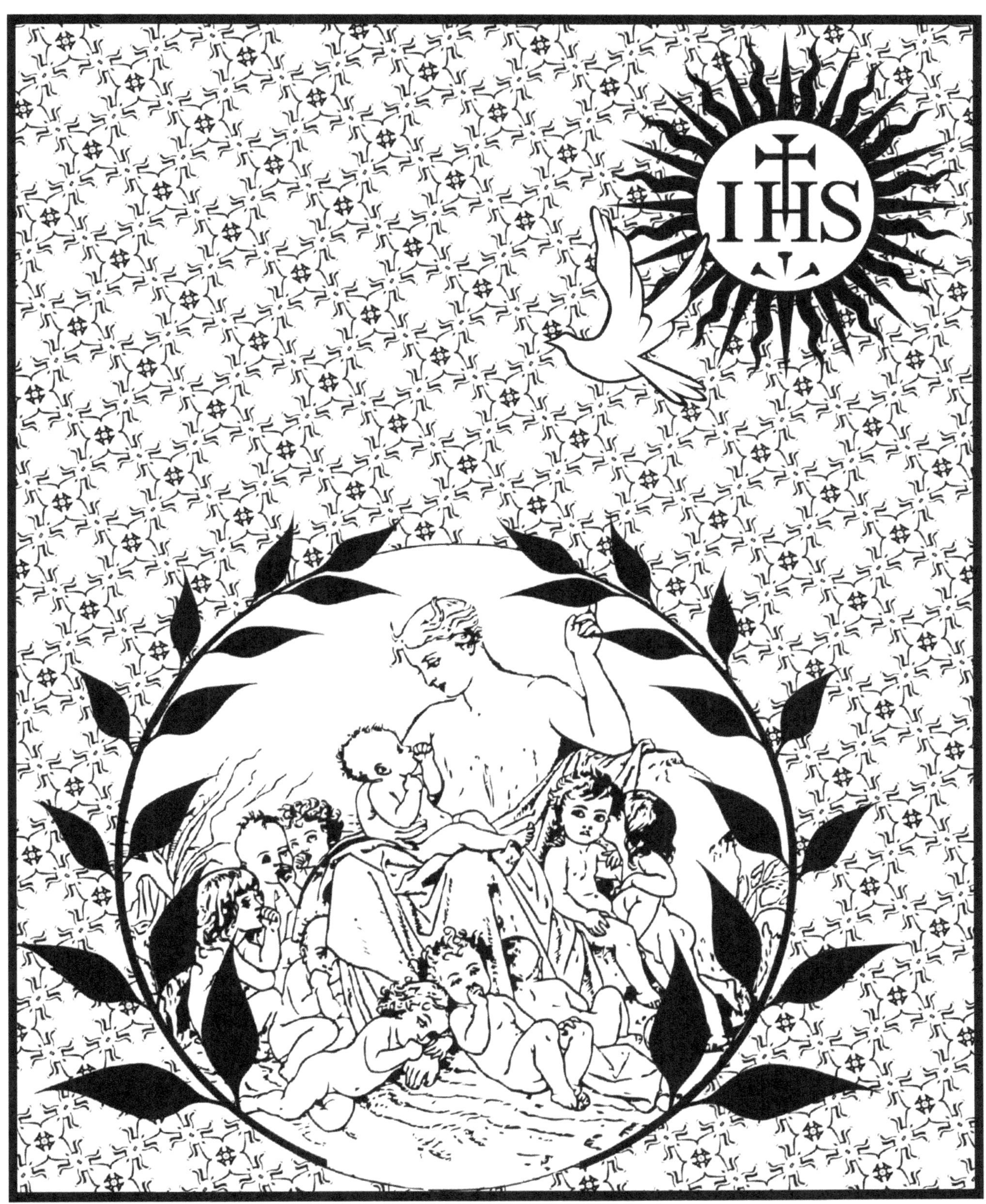

Blessed are the peacemakers, for they shall be called the sons of God.

Matthew 5:9

Further thoughts:

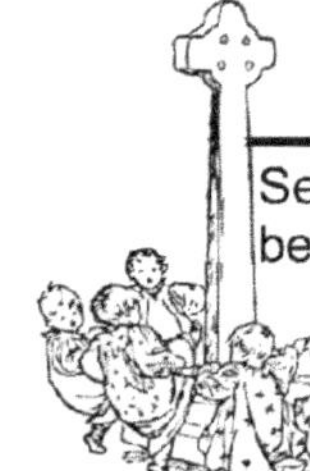

See what kind of love the Father has given to us, that we should be called the children of God; and so we are.

I John 3:1

What are the ideal characteristics of a father's love for his children?

How does God's love for us compare to the love of an earthly father?

What motivates our Father's love for us?

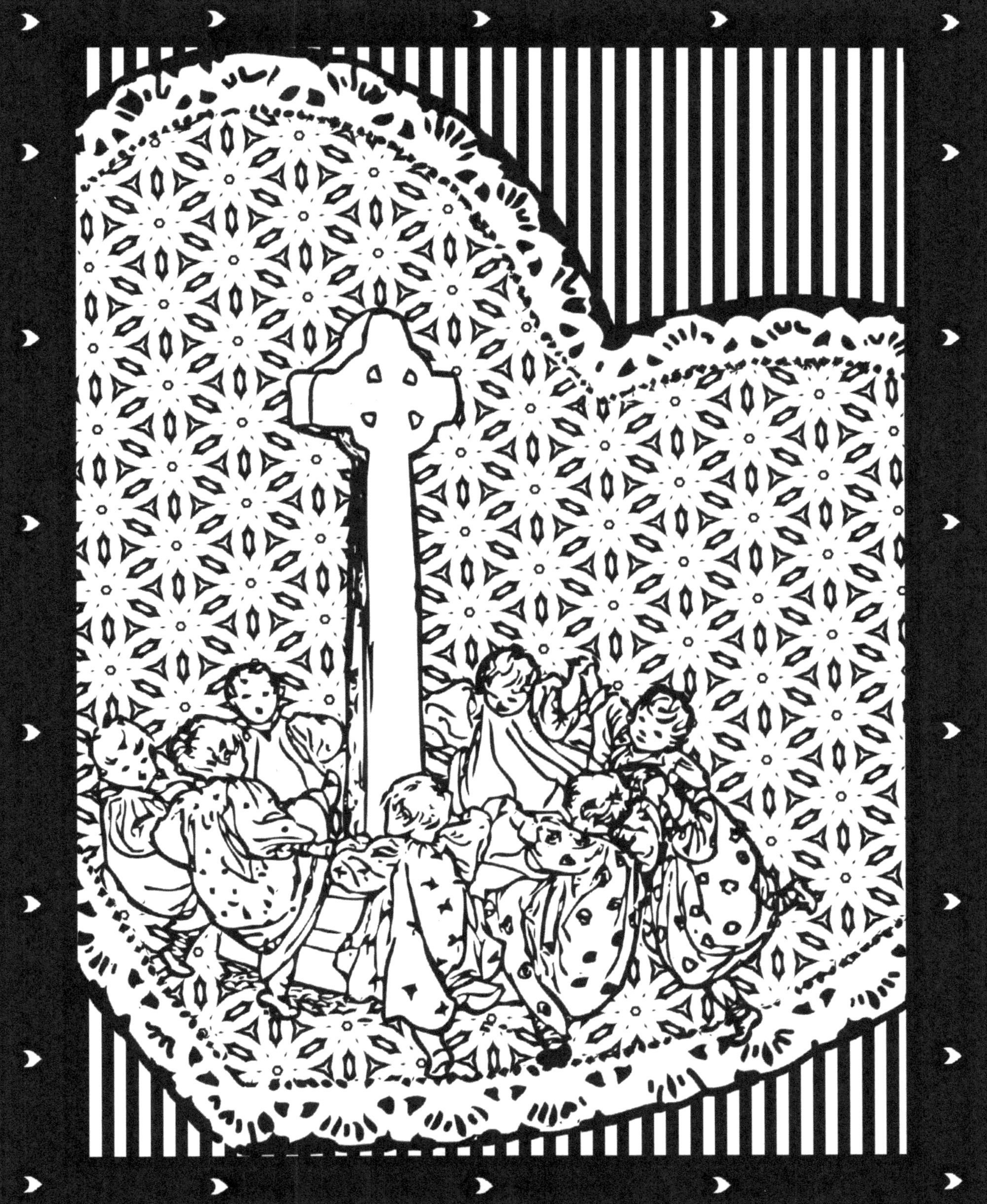

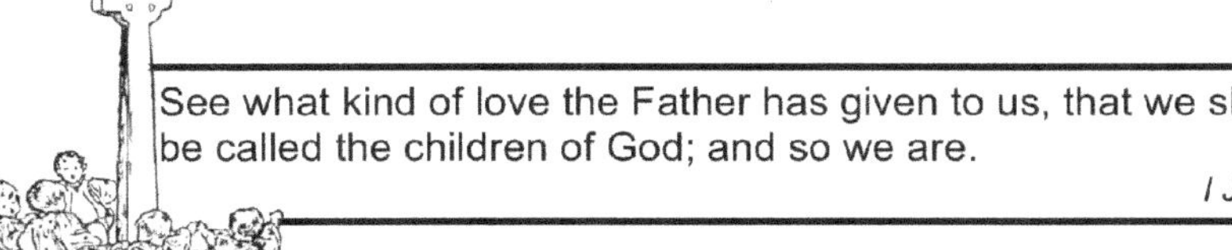

Further thoughts:

So far as it depends on you . . . what other factors - besides yourself - enter into an attempt to live peaceably?

Does this text in any way contradict or mitigate God's goal for us to be peacemakers?

Does this verse feel more realistic to you? Does it 'take the pressure off'?

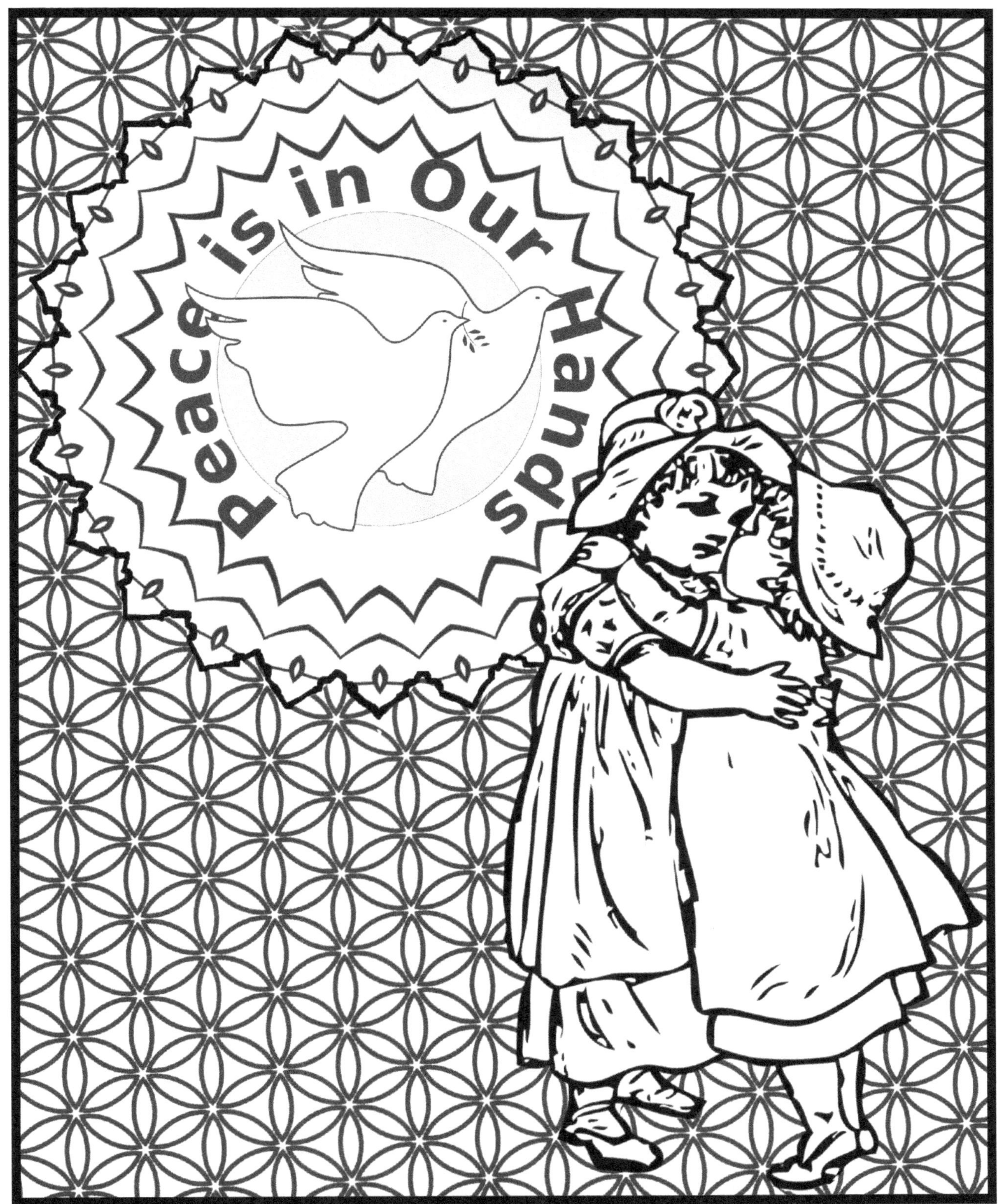

Peace is in Our Hands

> If possible, so far as it depends on you, live peaceably with all.
>
> *Romans 12:18*

Further thoughts:

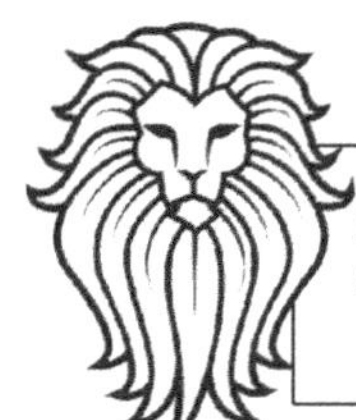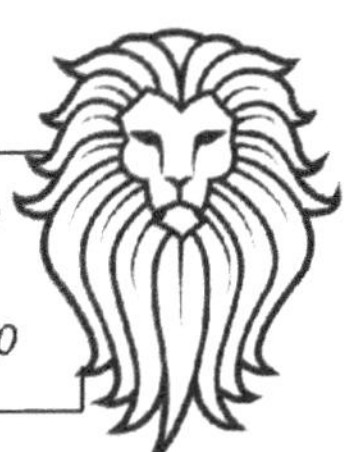

Blessed are those who are persecuted for righteousness' sake, for theirs is the kingdom of heaven.

Matthew 5:10

It's easy, in countries like America, to forget that persecution of Christians still exists today. List the countries that you know of where persecution goes on now.

Write the names of individuals that have recently died for their faith. (Google is a great resource.) Pray for the families and loved ones they left behind.

An old question - and a cliche - but still worth considering: If you were arrested for being a Christian, would there be enough evidence to convict you?

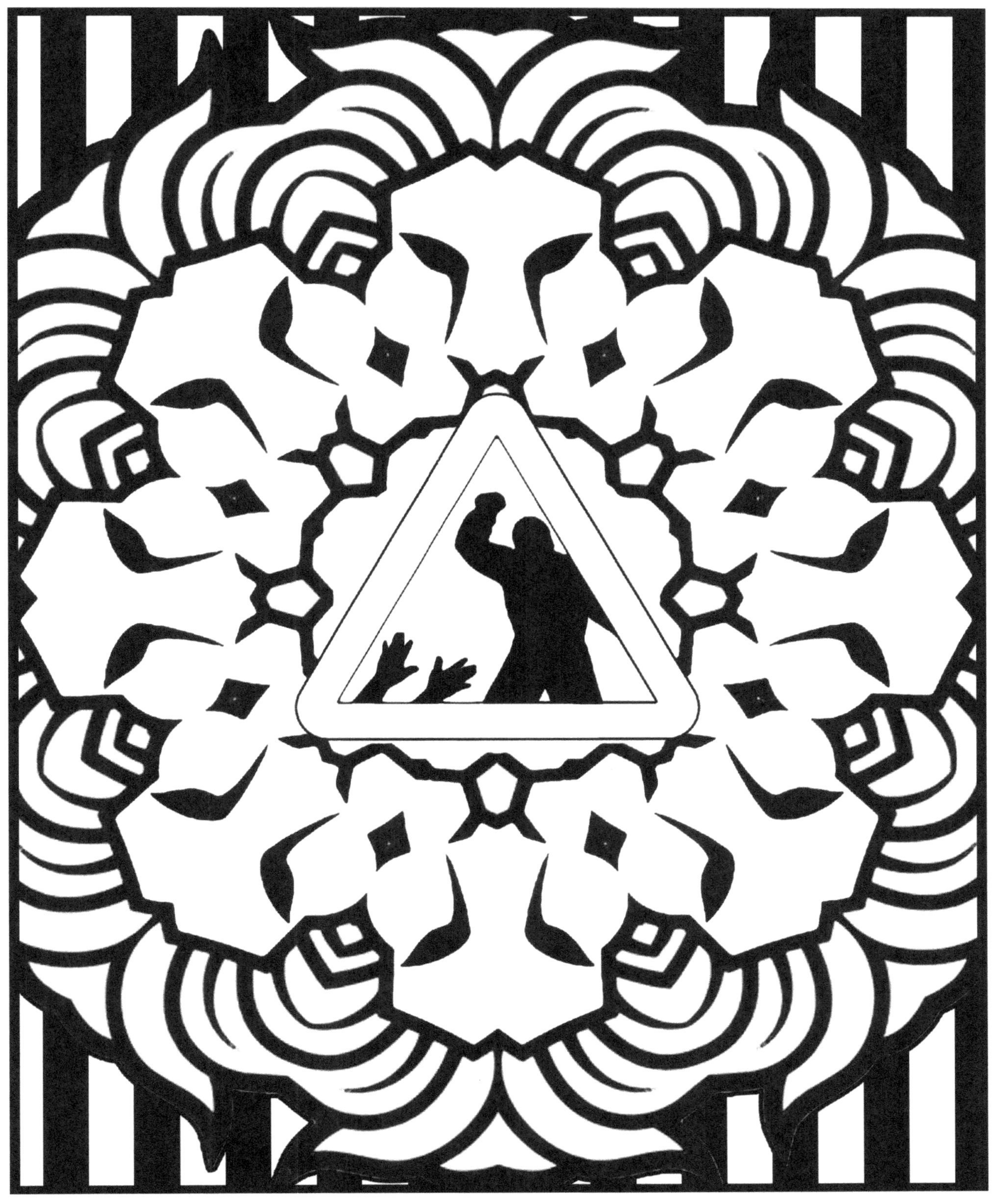

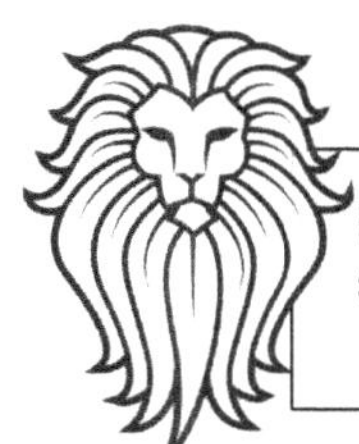

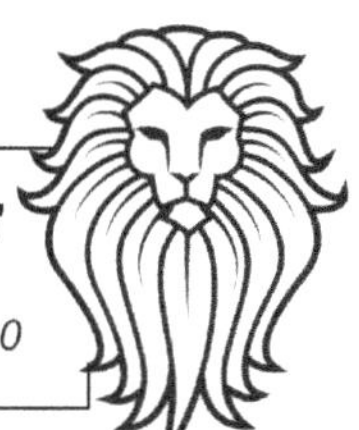

Blessed are those who are persecuted for righteousness'
sake, for theirs is the kingdom of heaven.

Matthew 5:10

Further thoughts:

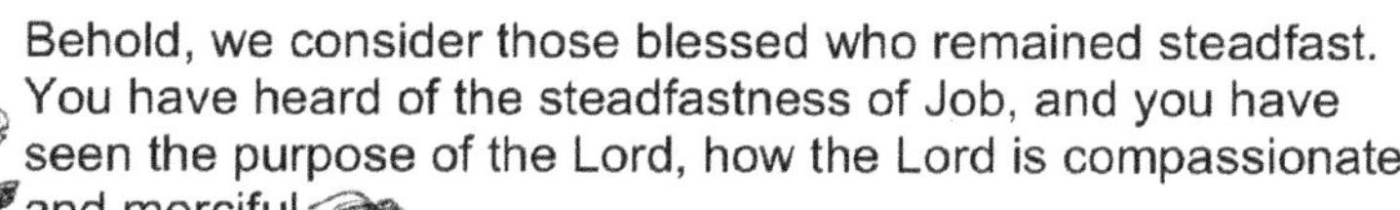

Behold, we consider those blessed who remained steadfast.
You have heard of the steadfastness of Job, and you have
seen the purpose of the Lord, how the Lord is compassionate
and merciful.

James 5:11

Have you ever been angry with God? How do you keep that anger from hardening into bitterness?

What did Job do when he finally confronted his anger?

All that Job lost was restored to him in his lifetime. Is this always the case? What part does faith play in maintaining a steadfast heart?

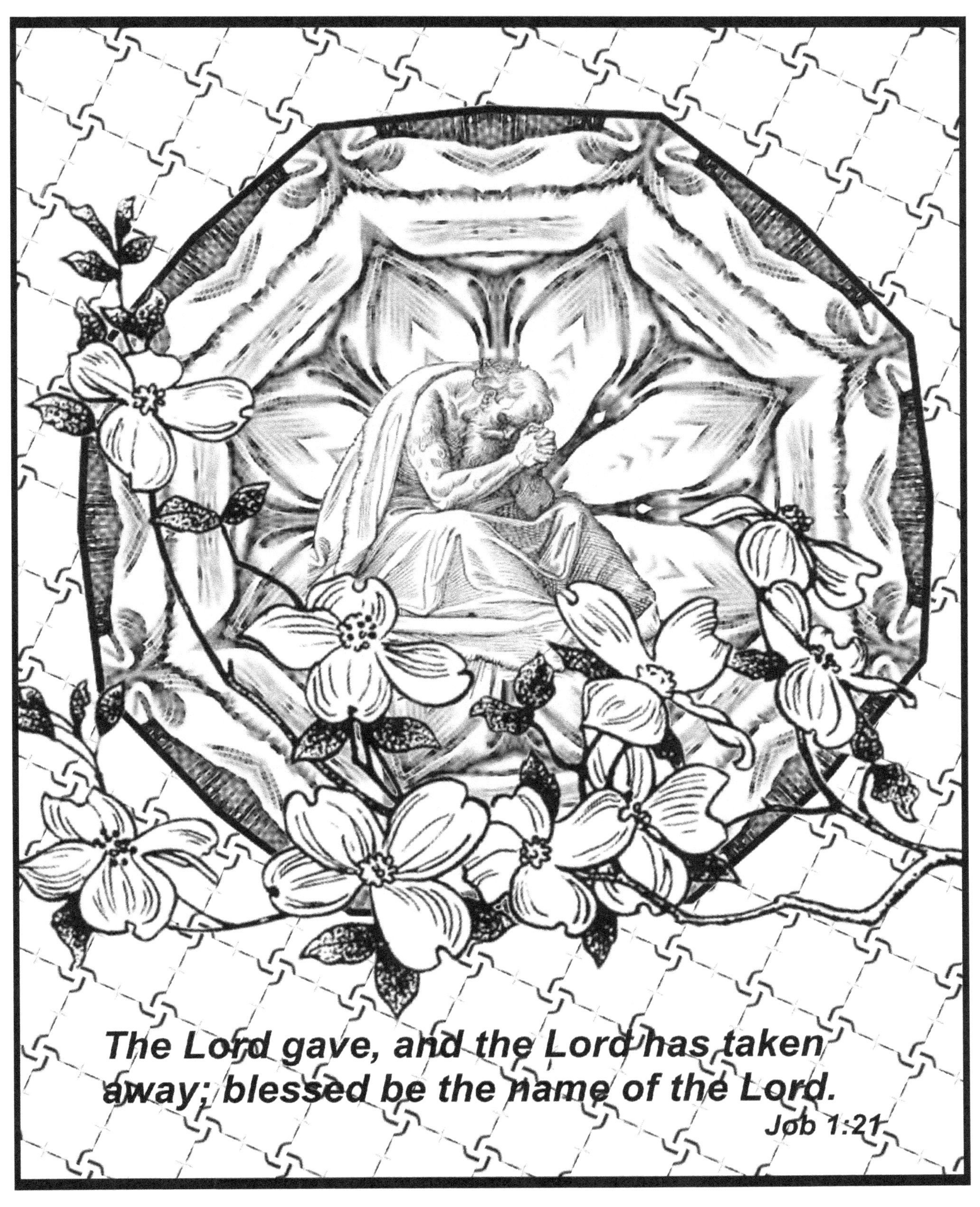

The Lord gave, and the Lord has taken away; blessed be the name of the Lord.

Job 1:21

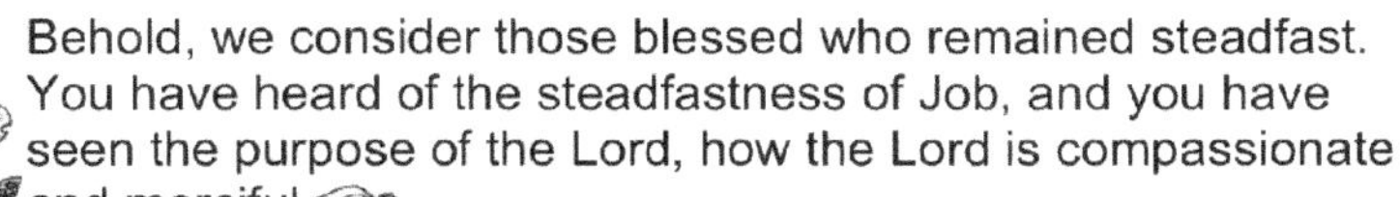

Behold, we consider those blessed who remained steadfast.
You have heard of the steadfastness of Job, and you have
seen the purpose of the Lord, how the Lord is compassionate
and merciful.

James 5:11

Further thoughts:

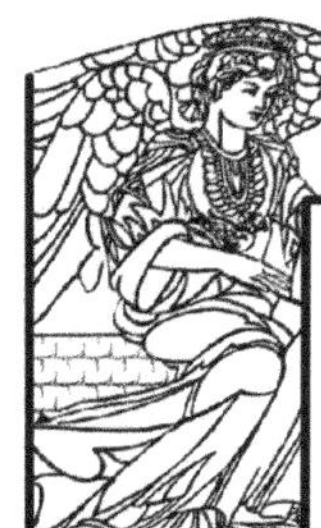

Blessed are you when others revile you and persecute you and utter all kinds of evil against you falsely on my account. Rejoice and be glad, for your reward is great in heaven, for so they persecuted the prophets who were before you.

Matthew 5:11-12

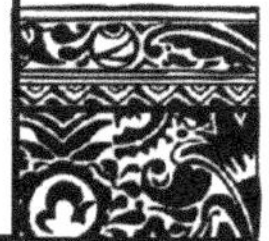

Do unbelievers have unrealistic expectations of professed Christians? Would this explain some of the assaults in the media against prominent believers who fall short of God's perfection?

Have you ever experienced attacks against your reputation because of your faith? How have you handled them?

Name all the prophets you can think of who were persecuted for their faith. How did they respond?

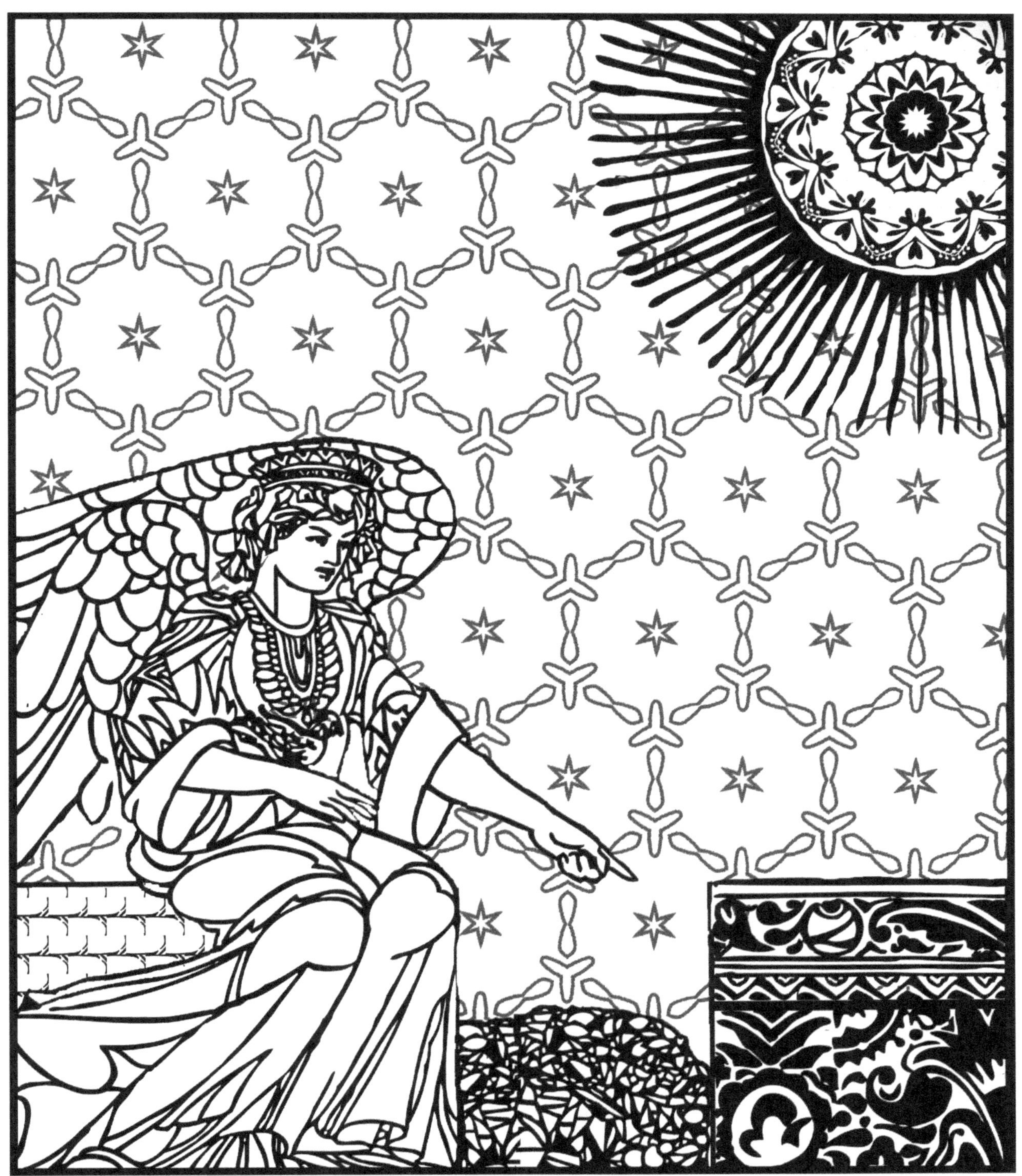

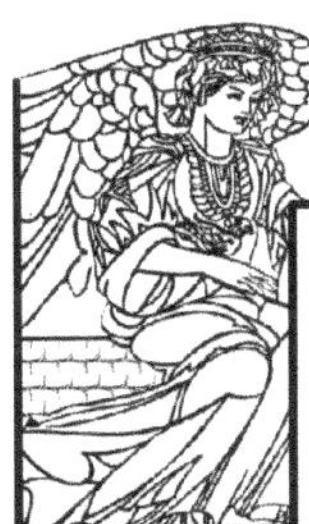

Blessed are you when others revile you and persecute you and utter all kinds of evil against you falsely on my account. Rejoice and be glad, for your reward is great in heaven, for so they persecuted the prophets who were before you.

Matthew 5:11-12

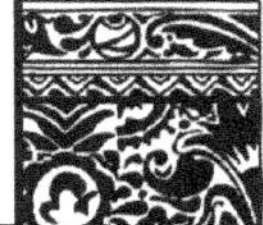

Further thoughts:

How do you define 'a little while?' Do you think God's definition might be different? Explain.

What does it mean to be called to his eternal glory in Christ?

God himself has promised to restore, confirm, strengthen, and establish you. Is this a promise He will fulfill in heaven? Or can we claim it for our lives today?

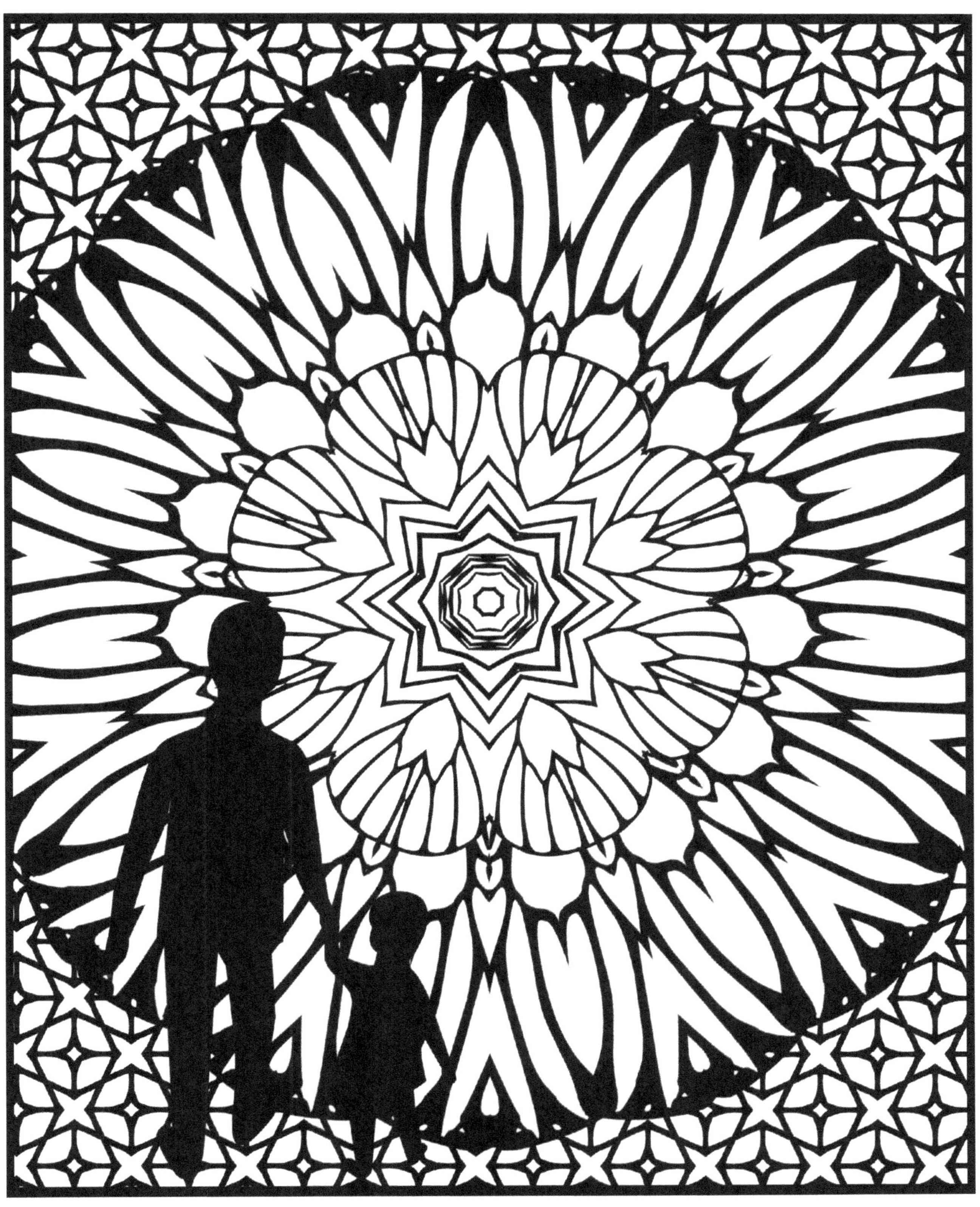

And after you have suffered a little while, the God of all grace, who has called you to his eternal glory in Christ, will himself restore, confirm, strengthen, and establish you.

I Peter 5:10

Further thoughts:

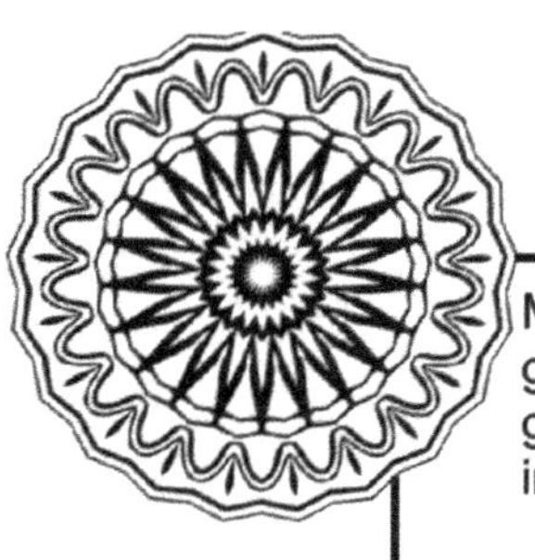

> May you be strengthened with all power, according to His glorious might, for all endurance and patience with joy, giving thanks to the Father who has qualified you to share in the inheritance of the saints in light.
>
> *Colossians 1:11-12*

This was Paul's prayer for the Colossian Christians - and is his prayer for us, as well. How many of these things do you need: strength, power, endurance, patience, and joy?

How have you been qualified to share in the inheritance of the saints?

Give thanks and praise!

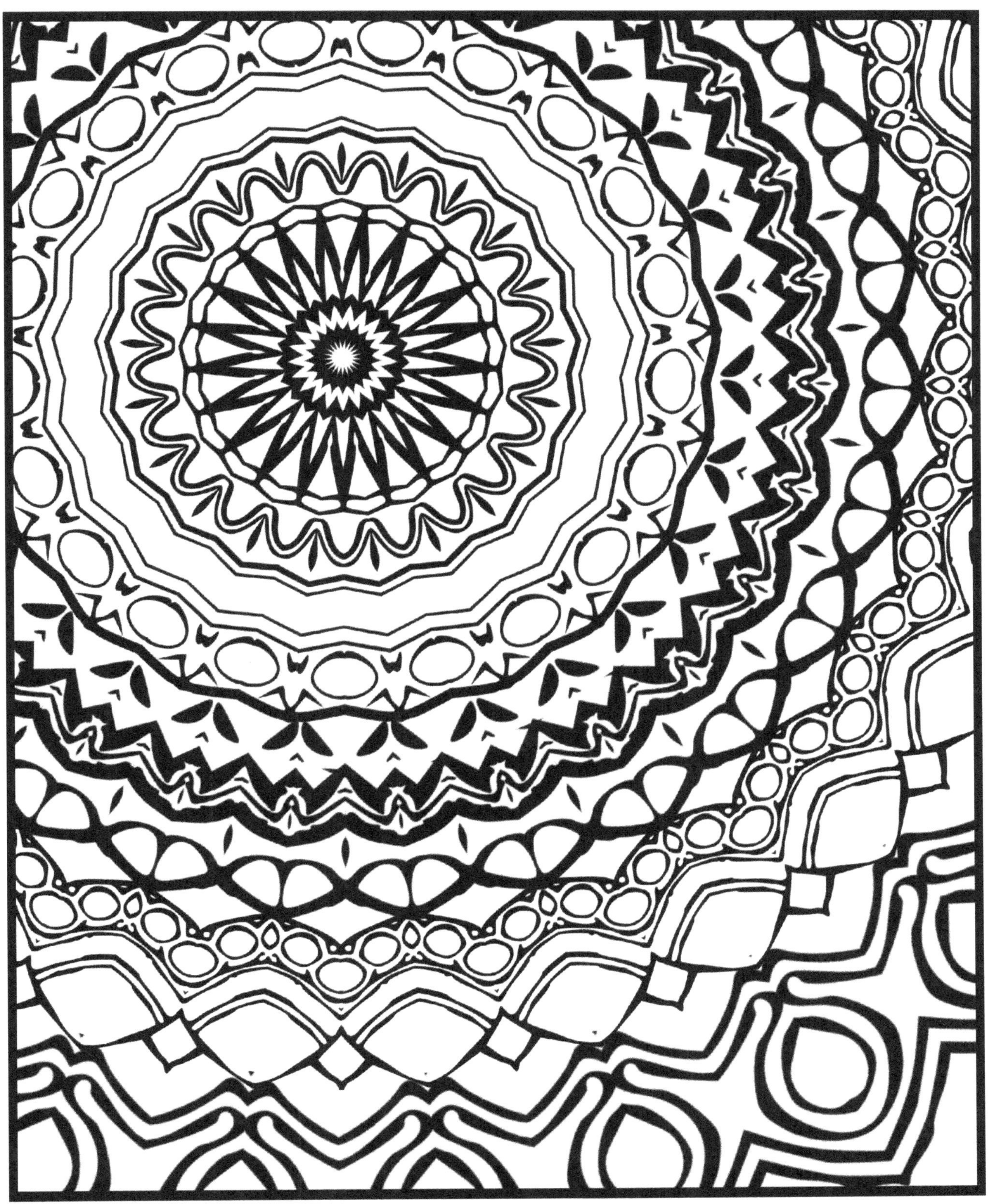

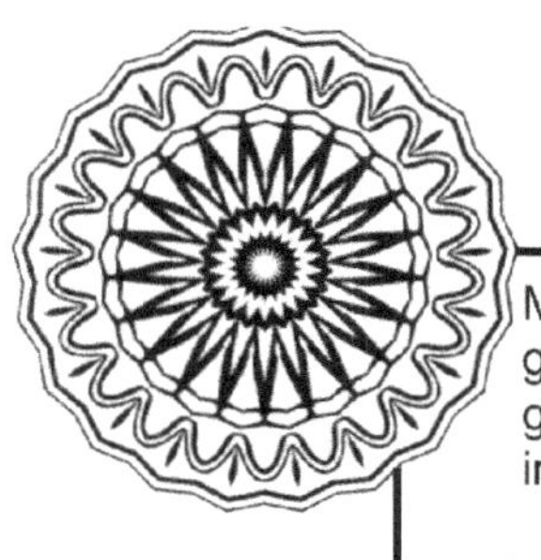

May you be strengthened with all power, according to His glorious might, for all endurance and patience with joy, giving thanks to the Father who has qualified you to share in the inheritance of the saints in light.

Colossians 1:11-12

Further thoughts:

Thank you for purchasing Blessed Be . . . I hope you've enjoyed your coloring journal experience! If you have five minutes to spare, please post a positive review on Amazon. Reviews help spread the word about books, and are really important to authors - especially newbies like myself! Thanks so much for your support.

Blessed be . . .
Isla

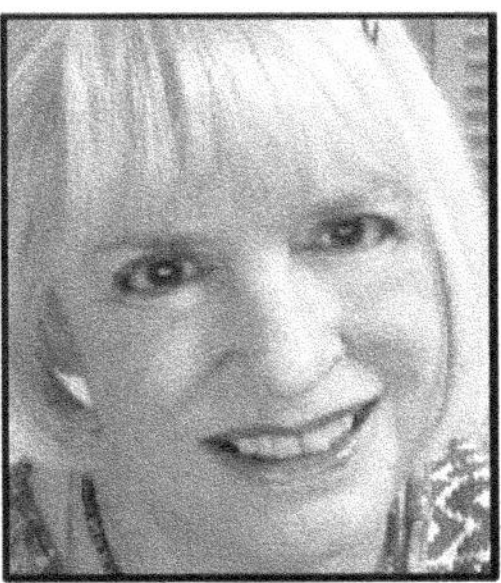

This is the first publication for Isla Backus, a native Houstonian now happily residing in Bend, Oregon. For more information, check out her website, IslaBackus.com. You can also find Isla on Facebook.

Coming soon . . .

A series of antique children's books with original illustrations converted to black and white images for adult coloring aficionados. Titles include:

- The Little Small Red Hen
- Wee Peter Pug
- Fiddle Dee Dee - by Eugene Field

And . . .

Two By Two - Coloring in Noah's Ark